Dear Barbara

Dear Barbara

ANSWERS TO THE
MOST-ASKED QUESTIONS
FROM TEENAGE GIRLS

Barbara Barrington Jones
WITH JANET THOMAS

Deseret Book Company • Salt Lake City, Utah

Library of Congress Cataloging-in-Publication Data
Jones, Barbara Barrington.
    Dear Barbara : answers to the most-asked questions from teenage
girls / Barbara Barrington Jones with Janet Thomas.
        p.   cm.
    Includes index.
    Summary: Uses letters the author has received from many different
young women to lead into advice on such topics of concern as self-
image, friendship, sex, parents, personal appearance and weight
problems, and especially spirituality.
    ISBN 1-57345-369-2 (pbk.)
    1. Teenage girls—Psychology—Juvenile literature.   2. Self-esteem
in adolescence—Juvenile literature.   3. Self-perception in
adolescence—Juvenile literature.   4. Sexual ethics—Juvenile
literature.   5. Beauty, Personal—Juvenile literature.   [1. Teenage
girls.   2. Conduct of life.   3. Christian life.   4. Self-esteem.
5. Letters.]   I. Thomas, Janet.   II. Title.
HQ798.J628   1998
305.235—dc21   98-10392
                                                                      CIP
                                                                       AC

Printed in the United States of America
10   9   8   7   6   5   4   3   2   1   8006 - 6362

To my mother, who believed in me and taught me

to have confidence in myself and to love God, and

to my father, who taught me about Jesus Christ

through his words and even more by his example.

They have both left me a legacy of love.

Contents

PART 4   LOOKING GOOD, FEELING GREAT

PART 5   MAKING GOOD CHOICES

Introduction

When I wrote my first book, *The Inside Outside Beauty Book,* I wanted to include my address in the back in case anyone wanted to write to me about anything that worried them. At first, my editors didn't want me to include my address.

"It could cause trouble," they warned.

"Do you really want girls writing to you?" they asked.

"Is it really a good idea?" they worried.

"Yes, I want it in," I said. I knew that some people who were reading my book might just need to talk to someone. I wanted to know what they were thinking about, what they were worried about. And I did get letters. Lots of them. Even though it was extremely difficult, I answered every one.

I also saved all those letters. Then, just before I started this book, I got my boxes out and, with some help, sorted the letters into subjects. This is what I found out. The two subjects people wanted most to know about were a tie: one-fourth, or 25 percent of the writers, wanted to know how to have higher feelings of self-worth or more confidence in themselves. Another 25 percent wanted some advice on how to lose weight and become more physically fit.

Then the next three subjects of interest were a three-way tie. At least 10 percent wanted to know about boys. Another 10 percent wanted to know more about improving their appearance. And another 10 percent wanted to know how to feel more spiritual and to be closer to Christ. The final short stacks of letters asked about making and keeping good friends, dealing with peer pressure and the Word of Wisdom, and improving relationships with parents.

As I wrote letters back, it made me think. What about other teens who might have these exact same problems and didn't know where to send a letter or were to afraid to write? Wouldn't they like to read some encouraging words?

That's how this book started. I have included just a few of the letters I have received, often with names and places changed to protect the privacy of those who wrote to me. In my responses to these letters, I've talked to girls about all sorts of challenges: dating, getting along with friends, dealing with parents, losing weight, getting to feel better about yourself, and other things that can really make your life better.

Usually it's not polite to read other people's mail, but in this case, it's more than all right. I hope you find some answers to questions you haven't dared ask. Or you may just find out that you're doing great.

I included my address in the back of this book, too. If you need to talk and you think I might be able to help, go ahead and write.

Part 1

Feeling Good about Yourself

Dear Barbara,
It seems like everybody I know is cuter or smarter or more popular than me. I wish I felt better about myself. Can you help?

You Are a
Masterpiece

I've heard it said that God is the master artist. Of course, it's easy to see the beauty he has created in rainbows, in mountain streams, in every bird and perfect flower. We can even see the beauty of God's power in the windswept isolation of a desert.

Just go outside and find any patch of grass. Sit down and take time to look slowly and carefully at every single bit of nature that you see from that one spot. Get down close to the ground and examine every insect, every blade of grass. Then look up at the sky. Notice every tree, the color of its leaves, the shape of each limb. In every single thing that the Lord has created is its own kind of beauty.

Now, stand up and go to the mirror. There before you is one of God's beautiful creations. Yes, you. There are no exceptions.

Look down at your fingers. There, at the tips of your fingers, is proof of the greatness of our Heavenly Father's artistry. Look carefully at the swirls and ridges on each finger. He gave each of us, every single person who is alive or who has ever lived or ever will live, a unique and completely different set of fingerprints. It's vivid evidence that God cares about each individual person. He has made billions of people and has never repeated himself. We are his treasures, his priceless creations. We are his masterpieces, each one individually signed by him.

I met a girl named Lillian Davis at BYU's Education Week a few years ago. She had attended some of my classes. Later she wrote me this letter:

Dear Barbara,

Thank you so much for your influence on me. Now I can look back at myself and say, "I've come a long way, baby." People, especially kids at my school, would make fun of me, calling me mean names. And you know what, I believed them. But now I just say, it could have been a lot worse. And someday, who knows when, I'll get married to a great guy who's loving and understanding. The one picture of me in this envelope is when I was in the 5th grade. The other is how I am today.

Here are the pictures that were in the envelope.

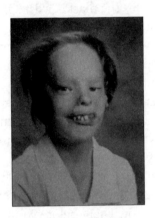 

I wrote Lillian and asked her if I could use her letter and her photos in my talks and in my book. This is the letter she wrote back:

Dear Barbara,

Thank you so much for responding to my letter, even though I

*can't remember exactly what I said in my letter. You have my full
permission to use anything you want.*

*In my life, nothing could get any better (except my hand-
writing). I just turned eighteen in November. I'm going to a drill
team formal with a guy I really like and I'm good friends with. I
just got a 3.87 on my report card, and I'm just plain happy.*

How did Lillian come to feel this way about herself? She felt the
presence of the artist, her Heavenly Father, with her. Lillian has had
to have many plastic surgeries over the years. She may even have had
a right to be angry, to feel like life wasn't fair, but she is happier than
99 percent of the girls who write to me. What is she going to accomplish by being so positive, by recognizing that God is with her and
has not abandoned her? She's going achieve some great things and
have a happy, beautiful life.

If God had wanted us all to look like the fashion models, he
could have made a few hundred thousand carbon copies. But he
didn't. He made each of us unique, with our own beauty. What a
remarkable artist the Lord is! And he will help you learn to see the
incomparable beauty of his creations, including the creation you see
in the mirror.

What Does Beauty Have to Do with Goodness?

Before we go any further, take a look at these two girls.

The girl on the left is Jodi Webb from Fruit Heights, Utah. She
really hates this picture. In fact, she's a little upset with me that I

Photo courtesy LPJ Photography

wanted to use it in this book. When she looks at this picture, she sees things that make her insecure. "I look fat. My face looks blotchy, and my hair is a poof. Also, my eyes are different sizes, and my ears always stick out so they need to be covered."

I can just hear you saying under your breath, "Oh, brother, this girl is *way* too hard on herself." I agree. When I look at her picture, I see the real Jodi. Look at the glow in her face, in her eyes, in her smile. It's no trick of the camera. It's not her makeup or how she fixes her hair. What Jodi is inside comes through loud and clear in this picture or in real life. She looks good because she is good.

The girl on the right is Greta Nelson from Salt Lake City, Utah. When this picture was taken, she had just been chosen to represent her area in the State Junior Miss program. If that were all you knew about her, you might think she had it made. But Greta is the third oldest of thirteen children. Her mother, whom she loved with all her heart, just died of cancer. Her father lost the wife he loved. Greta's little brothers and sisters have to grow up without their mother.

Now look at the picture of Greta. Can you sense the strength of her character? She had to face losing her mother at a time in her life when a young woman needs her mother most of all. When her mother was sick, she had to take over many of the household duties. She sat with her mother every day at her bedside and kept her involved in what was happening to each member of the family. Greta is pretty because she knows how to love.

What do these two girls have to do with each other? What happened when these two girls were together is the perfect example of what this book is all about.

As with all the advice in this book, the friendship between Jodi and Greta started with a letter. Sharlene Hawkes, a good friend of mine who was Miss America in 1985, wrote to me asking for my help. One of the things I have done for many years is help girls prepare in every way to participate in programs such as Junior Miss, Miss Teen USA, Miss USA, and Miss America. These girls, all in their late teens or early twenties, enjoy the opportunities these events provide them to perform their talents, develop their abilities to speak in public, gain confidence in social situations, and win college scholarships.

Sharlene, as director of the Junior Miss scholarship program for

Utah, knew of Greta, a young girl who needed someone to take a particular interest in her because she had recently lost her mother and wanted to participate in the program. She wrote this letter to me:

Dear Barbara,

One of my local directors recently called me to tell me about a participant in her local program who has been selected as a contestant for our upcoming Junior Miss scholarship program in February. This girl, Greta Nelson, is absolutely darling, but she is a diamond in the rough with an incredible story. It seems that she is the third oldest, age seventeen, in a family of thirteen children. Her father is a schoolteacher, and her mother just passed away in October from cancer.

Barbara, this girl could truly benefit with some help and attention. Do you know anyone here in Salt Lake who could possibly take her under their wing? Please call me.

Love, Sharlene

After I received this letter, I prayed about it. I simply did not have the time, and I didn't live in Salt Lake, but the Lord let me know in no uncertain terms that I was to help this girl personally. However, the only time that Greta could come to my house was the same week I had committed to helping Jodi Webb.

Jodi had been selected as Miss Utah Teen USA, and she was headed to the national pageant in a few months. We had arranged for her to come to my house for a week to prepare. If Greta came, it would have to be at the same time. How could we make this work? What I didn't realize then was that we were all being guided for a greater purpose. This opportunity for the three of us to work together for a week was an answer to prayer for us all.

When they arrived at my home, Greta was uncomfortable. I knew she would be likely be a little overwhelmed because she hadn't had much experience away from home, and on top of it she had just gone through such a traumatic experience with her mother's death. Immediately, Jodi did what she does best. She sensed that Greta's needs were greater than her own, and she began helping me teach Greta the things she needed to know. Jodi became Greta's friend and biggest supporter. We laughed hysterically as we taught Greta how to walk in high heels. We were in tears helping Greta prepare the tribute to her mother that she would perform as her talent. We took Greta to a secondhand clothing store and helped her put together an attractive wardrobe for her interviews and all other facets of her competition. In other words, Jodi gave all her energy and efforts in helping Greta be prepared to do her best.

Then Greta, who had come to love and appreciate Jodi, helped inspire her new friend to make the commitment to be and do *her* best.

And why did I need to see all this? I was right in the middle of writing this book. I had all these letters from young women just like Jodi, Greta, and you about their problems. I needed to focus with laserlike intensity on the things that will really make a difference in your life. I needed to see again that what I have taught and believed in for years is really true.

We are each created beautiful. Whether we appear so or not has little to do with how we look. It is within us. When we learn how to care for our skin, our hair, and our appearance, we are only caring for the things God has given us. More importantly, when we work to improve our attitude, our ability to make friends, and our unselfish devotion to others, we become beautiful in a way that is true and lasting. We become who we were always meant to be.

Chapter 2

I Just Want to Be Happy

You have heard people talk about ways to improve your self-esteem that will make you happy. Does it seem like an impossible problem? Maybe you say, "If I felt better about myself, I would be happier. But how can I feel better about myself when I'm so miserable? I can't just wake up one morning and say, Okay, today I'm going to feel great about myself." I admit, it doesn't work like that.

But I do know that self-esteem and feeling better about yourself are two sides of the Oreo cookie with a delicious filling of happiness inside. With one comes the other.

Here's a letter I received from a girl who wanted to know about being happy:

Dear Barbara,

I'm 5'11" tall, and I have size 10 feet. I've heard all the tall jokes until they're not funny anymore. The average girl at my school is about 5'6" and 115 pounds, and parties all the time. I dread even getting up in the morning. My sister and I have also not been getting along lately either. She's seventeen and I'm sixteen. She has a boyfriend and is very pretty, skinny, and used to be a model. I'm nothing like that, so I think I'm a little jealous. I wish I weren't so jealous because then there wouldn't be so many arguments all the time.

I'd like to ask you something if I could. I know that you're not a counselor or anything, but I was wondering: How do you learn to feel better about yourself? How do you feel more accepted by your peers and just be happy?

Love, Heidi

Dear Heidi,

There are so many things that I could tell you about learning to like who you are and learning how to be happier. The first thing that comes to my mind is a study done by the American Association of University Women. This organization sponsored a study to discover why people, especially girls, seem to lose their self-esteem as they grow up. This is a brief report of what they found out.

At birth, babies have 100 percent self-esteem. Does that even surprise you? Look where we came from. At our birth, we had just left our Heavenly Father and his complete and perfect love for us. Now, his love never changes even when we are away from him, but many things in the world start to cloud our vision. Even so, I'm confident that many of us can remember back to childhood when we felt complete self-worth.

This reminds me of a darling two-year-old girl I know, Bailey Jensen, who so far has kept that 100 percent self-esteem we've been talking about. Someone said to her, "You're so beautiful." Bailey replied, "Well, actually I've been told I'm gorgeous!" Now, that's 100 percent self-esteem.

In grade school, 67 percent of the boys still feel good about themselves, but the girls have slipped a little lower, to 59 percent. Then, in high school, 51 percent of the boys but only 24 percent of the girls still feel good about themselves. What happened? What caused the drop? And why is the girls' self-esteem so much lower than the boys'?

When I give these statistics to an audience of young women, they immediately know the answers. "We judge ourselves against other girls." "We look at some other girl and say, Oh, I wish I looked like her. I wish I had her hair, her skin, her body." "Models make us feel worse about the way we look."

I can tell you a few behind-the-scenes things about models. At one time I owned two modeling agencies. You would never know all the things those models go through to get that beautiful "natural" look. I laughed so hard one year when I was at the Miss USA pageant. The opening number was the song "I'm a Natural Woman." I looked up there at those girls with the fake eyelashes and tons of makeup, permed hair or hair extensions to make it longer and fuller, pads in all the strategic spots, glue to hold their swimsuits in place, blush on their legs, which are covered with tanning cream (the blush accentuates the muscle, making their legs look more shapely).

When you look, you see only the exterior of models. Do you know how much they starve themselves? Because they don't eat right, their skin gets broken out sometimes. Do you think they are always gorgeous and walk down the street looking like they do in the magazines? You wouldn't even recognize them.

I personally feel that most girls in the world could appear on the cover of *Seventeen*. The photographers and makeup artists can do all kinds of things with makeup tricks and hairstyles. In fact, a new business has spread throughout the United States: glamour photography.

You've seen those photographers in the mall. They can fix your hair and apply makeup thick enough to cover every imperfection. Then you are carefully posed, and the final shots are touched up. Look at these before and after pictures and you'll see what I mean.

But wait. Before you blame the models and photographers of the world for destroying the self-worth of young women, just stop and think. Designers and advertisers want their products or clothes shown to every advantage. It is eye-catching to see an attractive person, even one who does not represent the way real people look, modeling or demonstrating a product. They want us to look, and we do.

However, when we look and then feel inadequate or somehow of less worth, something else is going on inside us. Usually such feelings mean we have left the gifts that God has given us wrapped up tight, still sitting under the Christmas tree. It is time to unwrap them!

Let me give you an example of a gift that was misunderstood. Abigail Van Buren of "Dear Abby" fame told the story of a young man she called Bill who was graduating from high school. He and his father had shopped around for some time looking at cars; the family was wealthy, and a car was the customary graduation gift in Bill's neighborhood. Finally, the week before the big night, they found just the right car.

Think how surprised Bill must have been when he opened his graduation present a few days later and found, not car keys, but a Bible! He threw the book down in anger and left his father's house, never to return until he heard of his father's death. Later, while looking through some of his father's possessions, he found that Bible. He opened it, and in the front was a cashier's check for the price of the car he had hoped to receive.

When I read that story, I thought, "Stupid, stupid boy." Right? His father had given him a gift of everything he ever needed in his whole life. He had given him Heavenly Father's instruction manual on how to live our lives. Everything was in that gift, but the boy never opened it. If he had, he would have seen not only the value of that great gift but also that he would be given even the material possession that he wanted as well. He never knew until it was too late.

When you left your Heavenly Father's side to come to earth, your arms were literally piled high with gifts he was sending with you. Then, as you were growing up, chances are you started comparing your pile of gifts with everyone else's. Maybe it seems like all those other gifts look better and are more attractive than yours. But how will you know until you open them?

Find Your Gifts

My daughter Wendy is a good example of someone who has unwrapped her gifts and loves what she has found. In high school, Wendy was more interested in social activities than academic achievement. Although she was involved in lots of fun and worthwhile things, she never did make great grades all through high school. She definitely didn't want to go to college. She did love animals, though, and so she often said, "If only I could be a veterinarian."

Well, you can't become a veterinarian without a lot of college training. I encouraged Wendy instead to consider using the *gifts* that Heavenly Father had given her. She was so good at helping others do their makeup and hair attractively. She went to cosmetology school and made straight As. She won first-place awards at a hair show in Los Angeles. After graduating, she served a full-time mission. Besides teaching people the gospel, on her mission she did everyone's hair—elders, investigators, other sister missionaries—saving them a lot of money and helping them appear as neat and tidy as the Lord wishes his servants to be. And she made many friends as she shared all her talents.

Wendy honed her hair-styling skills on her brother, John, over the years

After Wendy returned home, she had to serve as an apprentice for two years. Using her skills, she was able to put her husband through school as he earned his master's degree. She now works in a professional salon and is very happy. I'm so proud of her because she found her gifts and put them to good use.

Be Practical and Logical

As we begin to explore our gifts, we may hope that a tiny talent may be something we can develop. Even though it is fun to dream about what might be, to truly put our talents to good use, we need to be practical.

Once when I was giving a talk in Australia a girl from the out-back (the outback is far away from the towns and cities, away from everything) came up to me and said, "I heard your talk about talents and everything. I want to be a model." In her case, looks had nothing to do with it: There is simply no such thing as being a model when you live in the outback of Australia.

In fact, her dream is not unusual. I have had many girls ask me how they can be models or actresses. I have to encourage them to be practical. Only a very few girls in the entire world will ever have a future in such a profession. You'll be happier and more satisfied if you look for practical things to do with your gifts.

Also while I was in Australia, I met David and Melinda Hunsaker, twins who were seniors in high school. Their family moved around a lot because their dad was in the mining business. David was an awesome wrestler. He told his dad, "This is my gift, my talent. I'm going to be a wrestler."

Photo courtesy Alan Carter Creative Photography

His dad was supportive, but his job required that the family move. The new high school didn't have wrestling, so David went into basketball. They moved again. The next high school didn't have wrestling or basketball. Were David's gifts wasted? No. While

14

he had been developing his athletic skill, he had also been playing the piano. He hated to practice, but his dad told him he had a talent for the piano. It was another gift from Heavenly Father.

When I met David, he had just composed an arrangement of melodies from both Australia and America for the entire orchestra to play at their high school graduation. He had written all the parts for all the instruments. It was an incredible use of his talents. He went to college and is majoring in music. He is now serving his mission in Russia. I'm sure the Russian people are feeling the Spirit through David's music. He was practical. When developing one gift turned into a dead end, he looked to another gift and other ways to develop his talents.

Don't Compare Yourself

Melinda, David's twin sister, played the piano too. She tried hard, but her talent was not on the same level as her brother's. She was good at the piano, but she did not have that spark of talent that would take her further. Melinda chose to take a homemaking class. As an assignment, the class members were asked to design something that represented the country they were from. Melinda designed a jacket that reminded her of the American flag. She sewed red, white, and blue striped leather together in a fun and imaginative way. The jacket was *incredible*. She even made the buttons by hand with clay in the shape of stars and painted them red.

Melinda also showed me a dress she had made for her sister. It had taken her only one day, and it was beautiful. What a talent!

Now Melinda is at Ricks College. She has found another outlet for her creativity. She is taking a specialized course of study in botany, learning about flowers and how to handle and arrange them. Someday she may be running her own flower shop. Like her brother, she has found a practical outlet for her talents. I'll bet that she will be one of those mothers who has her little girls all dressed up in darling clothes she has made herself.

Your gifts? Where are they? Look around. Sometimes you're stumbling right over your gifts because they are the things you take for granted. Sometimes they are the skills or abilities that come so easily to you that you don't pay much attention to them. What do you like to do? What are you good at? What interests you? These are the gifts that God has given you. In fact, what we are is a gift from God.

Heidi, unwrap your gifts, and it will begin to make you happy. Please let me know what you are doing with your gifts.

Love, Barbara

P.S. Don't forget what I just rambled on and on about. The important things in this letter are:

Look for your gifts! Your school counselors can even give you some tests to help you discover where your talents lie.

Be practical and logical! Find something that will help you earn a living. You never know what your future holds, and you'll probably need to make money somewhere along the line. You can't be a model if you live in the outback of Australia. You can't be a veterinarian if you don't make good grades, even if you do like dogs.

Don't compare yourself! We usually compare our weakest areas to someone else's strongest areas. How can you wish that you played the piano as well as Susie when she has been taking lessons for ten years and you have never had a lesson? Find what *you're* good at, and use it for all it's worth!

Chapter 3

Your Gift to God

In the last chapter, we talked about the gifts our Father in Heaven has given each of us. Now, when someone keeps giving you lots and lots of great presents, soon you want to start giving something back to that wonderful friend. We can, in fact, give a gift back to our Heavenly Father that will please him immensely. If what we are is God's gift to us, then what we become is our gift to him.

I received this letter from a girl who is now becoming a pleasing gift to God.

Dear Barbara,

I wrote to you several years ago as a confused teenager searching for happiness. I thought you would be glad to know that one of us struggling girls is turning out all right. I'm doing one of the best things that I've ever done in my life, and that is serving a mission! One thing that I have figured out over the years is that the times when I feel so lost and alone are the times when I'm relying on my own strength instead of relying on the Lord. Especially now while serving a mission, I have discovered that when I lose myself in service to others, I truly find myself and find true joy and happiness.

Now I need your help. One of our investigators is a teenage girl who is going though the same problems that I went through. She is so self-centered and can't see beyond herself, and she is miserable. I've told her all about you and want to ask you if you would please write her a letter like you did to me all those years ago. Her name is Martha.

Love, Sister Lunt

Dear Martha,

A friend of yours gave me your address and asked me to write to you. She didn't say too much about you except that you are not very happy with the way that your life is going right now. With this in mind, I want to tell you about a new theory I have recently discovered. It's called the light-bulb theory.

The light-bulb theory was developed by Dr. Gary Smalley. He says that if we had a light bulb just screwed into a socket which was attached to a long cord with a plug on the end, we would constantly be trying to find something we could plug into that would light up our lives. Sometimes we think happiness is like that. In other words, we are all searching for something to light up our lives and make us happy. We generally try to "plug into" three different things: people, places, and things.

Plugging into people. You may think that you will be happy if you have a boyfriend or a best friend. So, you find a cute guy and think that he is going to light up your life. And this is true for a while. Then an argument or two starts, and things aren't going well. Eventually you break up.

Maybe you and your best friend have been close for ages. Then she finds another friend and leaves you behind. That's when you find that true happiness doesn't really come from people.

Plugging into places. Maybe you think that travel or a vacation to a great place like Disneyland will light up your life. The trip is planned, the money is saved, and you are on your way. First of all, the plane is delayed. When you get to Disneyland, the lines are a mile long, and it is broiling hot. *Space Mountain* makes you sick to your stomach, and *Pirates of the Caribbean* is closed for renovations.

The day is not what you thought it would be. Now you realize that places will not bring you happiness.

Plugging into things. Things sometimes seem to be quick avenues to happiness. If you only had that new outfit for the first day of school! That would make you happy. You work and work until you save enough to buy the outfit. On the way to school that first day, your little brother gets grease on the car seat and you sit in it. Then, in the cafeteria, you accidentally spill red drink on your outfit. Now you have a lovely red stain on the front and grease on the back. You wash it as soon as you get home, and you get the stains out, but your great new outfit is starting to go limp and hang funny. You wear it for the next few months, but before long that outfit is not lighting up your life anymore.

The true light. What *truly* lights up our lives is the fact that we were born with the light of Christ (see D&C 84:46; 93:2). Instead of looking for a light source outside ourselves, one that will always eventually fail, we need to use the light we were born with—the light of Christ. And true happiness comes when the light flows down through the cord and out to others. It's called service or good works.

This reminds me of a story that the famous novelist Pearl S. Buck wrote about Rob, a fifteen-year-old boy growing up on a farm. His father woke him every morning at four so he could help milk the cows. The boy just hated getting up that early. A few days before Christmas, Rob overheard his father telling his mother that he wished he did not need Rob's help so much because his son was always so deeply asleep in the mornings. He wished he could let him sleep.

Hearing those words, Rob suddenly realized that his father loved him. They hadn't talked much about love in their family. The farm took so much time and effort that they didn't seem to need such words. To Rob, the discovery of his father's love was a miracle of new awareness. He suddenly wished he had been able to save more money to buy a better present for his father than the necktie he had purchased at the discount store.

On Christmas Eve, Rob lay in his bed in his attic room, looking out his window. The stars seemed much brighter than they usually did. They reminded him of the star of Bethlehem. Then it came to him. The stable was like their barn, but it was good enough for the shepherds, Mary, Joseph, and the baby Jesus.

Then Rob had the most wonderful idea. He thought of the gift he could take to a barn for the man who he loved most in the world. He would get up early, earlier than 4:00, and he would creep into the barn and get all the milking done. He would do it alone, milk the cows, strain the new milk into the milk cans, and clean up. Then when his father went in to start the milking, he would see that it all had been done.

Rob laughed to himself. It was the very thing for him to do, but he must not sleep too soundly. He woke himself up time after time, afraid to do more than doze. Finally, at a quarter to three, he got up, quietly dressed, and crept downstairs.

Rob had never milked all alone before, but it seemed almost easy. He kept thinking about the surprise on his father's face. His father would come in and call him as usual, saying that he'd get things started while Rob was getting dressed. He would go to the barn and look for the milking cans, but they wouldn't be there. They would already be standing in the milk house, filled.

Rob smiled as he milked. Two strong streams rushed frothing into the pail. Milking for once was not a chore. It was something else, a gift to his father who loved him.

When Rob finished, he poured the milk into the cans and covered them, washed the pan, put everything away, closed the milk house, and crept back upstairs. He could hear his father getting up. Soon his father opened the door of his room.

"Rob," his father called. "We have to get up, son, even if it is Christmas."

"All right," Rob said sleepily.

"I'll go out," his father said, "and get things started."

The door closed, and Rob lay still, laughing to himself. In just a few minutes, his father would know.

"Rob, son . . . you . . . " His father was laughing, a queer, sobbing sort of laugh. "Thought you'd fool me, didn't you." His father was standing beside his bed, feeling for him in the dark, pulling away the covers.

"It's for Christmas, Dad." He found his father and clutched him in a great big hug. He felt his father's arms go around him. It was dark, and they couldn't see each other's faces.

"Son, I thank you. Nobody ever did a nicer thing."

"Oh, Dad, I want you to know . . ." He didn't know what to say. His heart was bursting with love.

"Well, I reckon I can go back to bed and sleep," his father said after a moment. Just then they both heard the rustling of the younger children waking up. "Come to think of it, son, I've never seen you children when you first see the Christmas tree. I was always in the barn. Come on, son."

Rob got up, pulled on his clothes again, and went down to the Christmas tree. Oh, what a Christmas! His heart nearly burst with shyness and pride as his father told his mother and the younger children how Rob had gotten up all by himself. "The best Christmas gift I ever had, and I'll remember it, son, every year on Christmas morning so long as I live."

Rob gave his father the best thing he had to give—himself. He used the knowledge his father had taught him to be in his father's service. It was the perfect gift, to use the talents his father had helped him develop in a way that made his father both proud and pleased. Our Heavenly Father feels the same way about us. When we are in his service, using the talents he has given us, he cannot receive a better gift from us.

Over the years I've discovered that one of my gifts is teaching. I'll never forget the time a Young Women's president in a tiny town in New Mexico asked me to come and speak to her girls. The town was so small and so remote that they hardly ever had any speakers come. We had to set the date quite far in the future, but they were willing to wait.

The day finally came for me to travel to New Mexico. I had to fly from San Francisco to Los Angeles, then catch a smaller commuter plane to Flagstaff, Arizona. But the flight was delayed in San Francisco. I knew I was going to have trouble making my connection in Los Angeles. I remember rushing off the airplane and asking the airline representative where I needed to go. She told me to go down the hallway to a big statue, then go down the stairway, and at the very end, I would see the exits going out onto the runway where the small planes were loading.

I ran as fast as I could down to the statue, down the stairs, and up to the counter. The woman there told me they were just barely closing the airplane doors. I looked outside. Workers were just wheeling the stairs away from the door of a small plane. The woman at the counter ran out and yelled that they had one more passenger. They pushed the stairs back, and I ran up to the door and told the stewardess I had just landed on a flight that had been delayed and wondered about my luggage. She told me that it would be impossible for my luggage to have been transferred to this flight.

I sat in the very back of the plane and started thinking. My luggage contained not only all my visual aids for my presentation but my clothing, makeup, curlers—all my "girl necessities." More importantly, even my migraine medicine was in the luggage. That was the first time I had ever put my migraine medicine in my suitcase. I usually carried it with me. But I had been in a hurry and had thrown it in my bag. Without my medicine, I was guaranteed to wake up with a migraine, and I would likely end up in the emergency room of the hospital.

So I prayed. I told my Father in Heaven that he knew how long those girls had been waiting for this event. He knew how I wanted to serve him. I needed his help. I told him I trusted that he would provide a way for me to pursue the gifts he had given me.

I think my faith came to the rescue as I remembered this scripture: "Trust in the Lord with all thine heart; and lean not unto thine own understanding. In all thy ways acknowledge him, and he shall direct thy paths" (Proverbs 3:5–6). I just put it in his hands, knowing he would not fail me.

When I got off that plane and walked into the one-room terminal and saw the smiling Young Women's president and her counselors, I was so pleased to be there. As we greeted each other, I glanced to the side—and there was my luggage! I knew that Heavenly Father had performed a miracle. There seemed to be no way my luggage could have been taken from the first plane and made it to the second.

God does hear our prayers when we are serving him. And service does bring us happiness (and sometimes miracles). I had everything I needed that day to be able to help those young women gain a better understanding about being daughters of a Heavenly Father who loved them, who wanted them to learn ways to feel better about themselves.

Another Miracle

Let me tell you about one more miracle. I was scheduled to go to Mexico on a speaking trip with Brad Wilcox. Brad had taken a group of student teachers down to Mexico and placed them in schools where they would be teaching in Spanish. We were to present a series of lectures together to them.

The night before I was to leave, Brad called and told me his group had taken some clothing down with them to give to the small children at an orphanage. The children were thrilled to have clothing from the United States. But some teenage girls were also living at the orphanage. Brad said his group hadn't known about the girls and hadn't brought any clothing for teenagers. He had observed as the older girls in the orphanage had stayed on the outskirts watching. They had smiled because they were pleased for the younger children, but he saw in their eyes the wish that they had been included.

Brad, out of his great love and concern, called me to see if I could get some teenage clothing together and bring it with me. It seemed impossible. It was late in the evening. I had to leave early the next morning, and I hadn't even packed my own suitcase. I prayed and told Heavenly Father that Brad meant so well, but only with the Lord's help could I possibly do this.

I called one of my closest friends. She called the Young Women's president in our stake. They got their hotline going. The next morning I found two boxes of clothing on my doorstep. These were not small boxes, and they were filled to the top with wonderful clothes. Some things even still had price tags on them.

I threw the boxes in the car. When I arrived at the airport, I was told I had too much luggage to check in. I would have to pay $55 per box for excess luggage. I didn't have that much extra with me for these boxes. I went to the counter, praying the whole way. I told the woman the whole story of why I had these two extra boxes. She told me they would just ship them through without charging me.

When I arrived in El Paso, Texas, the area president of the LDS Church met me at the airport with his counselors. They told me I couldn't take the clothes across the border. Although there was nothing illegal about carrying donated clothing, the boxes would likely be confiscated because they weren't my personal clothing. The Mexican customs officials would take the items to sell themselves and pocket the money.

We had the idea to repack all the clothes in grocery sacks. If the officials opened the trunk and saw only grocery sacks, maybe they wouldn't be interested enough to look inside.

Before we came to the border, we pulled off to the side of the road and said a prayer, then got back into the long line. If we were lucky, we would be waved across the border without a car check. When asked about our citizenship, we told them we were Americans. They just waved us through!

As we crossed the border, we just looked at each other. Yes, God loves us and hears our prayers, we all knew. We met the head of the orphanage and handed over the clothing. It wasn't too much later that we got a note from him saying that we wouldn't have believed how those teenage girls reacted when they saw those beautiful clothes. They were so happy. It was Christmas in September.

Oh, the blessings and happiness we felt. I sent a copy of the note to the Young Women's president who had collected the clothing and told her the story. I asked her to share it with her Young Women. When I saw her later, she told me: "You'll never know how happy my girls were when I read them your note on Sunday. How great they felt to be a part of this great act of service."

Yes, serving does bring real happiness. Find your talents and gifts. Work on them. Then use those gifts. That will be the finest gift you can give to your Father in Heaven. And the funny thing about it is, when you give away your gifts in service, you feel the greatest happiness you will ever feel.

Even though I haven't met you, I just know you can help make a difference in other people's lives. You have a great friend in Sister Lunt. She loves you. I hope we have a chance to meet someday.

Love, Barbara

P.S. Don't forget the light bulb theory: People, places, and things will not make you happy or light up your life. You already have the light in you, the pure light of Christ. It is only when that light within you goes down through the cord and out to other people in service that you will find true happiness. And when you are in the Lord's service, using the talents he has given you, you cannot give a better gift to him.

Chapter 4

The Personality Plus Factor

What do you think about when someone says, "She has a really great personality"? Right now: think of a person you know who has a fabulous personality. What does this person have that you like so much?

When people with personality talk, you listen. They make you laugh. They make you feel enthusiastic about whatever you are doing. It's fun to be with them. How do they do that? Do they have tricks?

No, they don't have tricks. We all have certain personality traits. Some people just don't have a shy bone in their bodies. Some are quiet, but are great listeners. Others seem to have a special sensitivity in understanding feelings. Some have lots of energy. Many are quick to laugh and see the fun in the world around them. All of these things are wonderful personality traits. But all great personalities have one thing in common—a positive attitude.

Your attitude is one thing that is in your complete control. By having a positive attitude, you can change your situation from horrible to wonderful. That's the Plus Factor. Take your own great personality (yes, you already have a great personality), add the plus of a positive attitude, and you won't have to envy anyone.

Please read this letter a girl wrote to me:

Dear Barbara,

My name is Katherine, and I am fifteen years old. I am the oldest child of six. One of the biggest problems I have in my life is self-esteem. My self-esteem is pretty low. I constantly compare myself to others, especially my friends. My friend Jennifer has short, thick, beautiful, full, blonde hair. Her eyes are a stunning blue. She almost always looks perfect. Her smile (even with braces) is positively outrageous.

I constantly compare myself to her, saying, "If my hair weren't so red, it would be better," or "If my eyes were bigger and more blue, I'd be prettier," or "If my smile were wider or my teeth were bigger . . . " The list goes on forever. I'm very short. I don't like my height. I always wish I could be taller. I also have a weight problem. Sometimes I blame that problem on my height and say, "If I could grow five inches, I'd be a lot slimmer." But I know I've stopped growing, so I'll never be any taller.

One of my goals in life (aside from marrying in the temple) is to feel good about myself and love myself as the Lord commanded me. It is hard for me to try to accomplish this. I really need help. Is there anything you think I should do that would help me? If you have any advice to give me, I would appreciate it so much!

Love, Katherine

Dear Katherine,

It made me feel so sad when I read your letter. In every sentence you were tearing yourself apart for something you didn't have or another thing you wished you did have. *Remember that you will become the person that you think you are seeing in the mirror. If you keep telling yourself all the negative things, you will eventually become a negative person.*

I can really relate to you, because when I was your age, I was 5'10" and wanted to be shorter. My mom would say, "Barbara, you can't go on a diet and lose three inches off your height. You have to accept the height you are." I hated wearing a size 10 shoe, but I couldn't chop off my toes in order to fit into a size 7. I hated that I had a figure just like a sausage. I wanted a long, narrow waist. But I have about a three-inch space between my rib cage and my hip bone. They call that being short-waisted. Even if I lost 100 pounds, I would never have a long, tiny waist. I wanted to have a nice "chest," but I was what people refer to as flat. Yuck!

Why couldn't I just be normal like everyone else? Every time I looked in the mirror, there was something I wanted to change about myself. But, Katherine, every time we pull ourselves down, we are painting another layer on an ugly mask that we are creating for ourselves. In other words, we are reinforcing over and over again those qualities that we wish we didn't have.

I want to tell you a fairy tale, a story with a prince and a princess. It's called the *The Happy Hypocrite*. It was written by Max Beerbohm, but I'm just going to tell it in my own words.

Once upon a time there was an ugly lord named Lord George Hill. He fell madly in love with a beautiful princess, but his face was so grotesque she wouldn't have anything to do with him. Then Lord Hill came up with a plan. He went to the local mask maker and paid him a fortune to create a wonderful mask of a handsome prince. He could hardly wait to hurry back to the palace and slip it over his own ugly features. But, hey, something still wasn't right. He decided that if he looked like a handsome prince, he'd better start acting like one.

When he presented himself to the princess with his mask in place and acting like a prince, she fell madly in love. They were married and lived happily every after.

Well . . . not exactly. They did live happily for many years, until a miserable villain discovered the well-kept secret. This traitor ran into the throne room and r-i-p-p-e-d off the mask.

The princess gasped. Lord Hill threw his hands up to cover his face. But there was no need. In all those years of acting like a handsome prince, he had literally turned into the person he wanted to be.

That can happen to you. You have a choice about how you relate to other people. You can make a conscious choice to see the good in your life and in yourself. Be positive, and positive things will happen to you.

The Worst Year Ever

My daughter Wendy's junior year of high school was a horrible year. It started out when I took her to a beauty salon just before school started in the fall because she really wanted a new way to wear her hair. When it was cut, Wendy turned to me with tears in her eyes and, with the hairdresser standing right there, cried, "I hate it! She's ruined me!"

I picked her up after the first day of school. Before she even sat down in the car, she was complaining bitterly about every single teacher and most of the students in her classes. I hoped her unhappiness would blow over in a few days. It didn't.

Wendy did like one guy, but he never asked her out. Another guy took her out, and he was okay, but when the Christmas formal came, neither one of them asked her. Wendy didn't get to go at all, and that confirmed her worst fears. "I told you this would be the worst year ever," she cried.

Soon after this fiasco, Wendy's good friends Jason and Andrew were traveling to a game where Wendy was cheerleading. They were involved in a terrible car accident, and both were killed. Wendy was devastated. She was upset and angry, mad at the situation and at the world. I may be wrong, but deep down I had the impression she was even angry with God.

As Wendy's junior year came to an end, her dad suggested it would be healthy for her to get away. We had a terrible time talking her into trying anything, but her dad thought it would be good for her to spend the summer with Teen Missions International, a youth service group of thousands of teenagers going worldwide to do work projects for the needy. Wendy's team was going to New Guinea.

Wendy was furious. She wasn't going to go. She said, "If I jump off the balcony and break my leg, do I still have to go?" Her dad said, "You'll go on crutches, but you have to go." She refused to pack and get ready. Her attitude was terrible, but we were desperate to help her find something that would get her out of herself.

After a month of army-like training in the Everglades of Florida, Wendy and her group flew to Australia and then to New Guinea, where they were loaded onto trucks and driven over bumpy roads for forty-eight hours. When they got to the bank of a river, they transferred to canoes for an eighteen-hour trip to the primitive village where they would live and work. By this time, these young people were beyond exhausted. They had jet lag, truck lag, and canoe lag. They wanted desperately to crash in soft beds and sleep for days, but the only sleeping accommodations available were sleeping bags on hard ground in flimsy tents.

Rain poured down in bucketfuls. It was suffocatingly hot, over 120 degrees. And the only shoes they had been allowed to bring with them were one pair of heavy work boots. In the weeks that followed, Wendy's boots were completely worn out.

Wendy's team helped build a hospital and a bridge. They had no machinery, so everything had to be done by hand. She worked harder than she had ever done before in her life. The team woke at dawn and stopped only long enough to eat during the long, hard day. If they didn't hustle, they would hold up the work of other groups.

Wendy recalls: "At night, I wanted to cry, but I was too tired. The tears just wouldn't come. I had blisters that were sore and broken. My back hurt, and my muscles ached. I was covered with mosquito bites. I never dreamed life could be so hard."

So it went, day after day, until one afternoon, while timbers for the bridge were being moved, a huge log slipped and crushed the hand of one of the team members. The girl screamed in pain. Blood was everywhere.

Quickly the group gathered around and hoisted the heavy wood off their friend's hand. Adult supervisors called on the shortwave radio for a helicopter, and the injured girl was flown out to receive medical help.

The team members who remained behind were tired beyond words. They were sore, dirty, covered with sweat, and desperately worried about their friend. They could have said: "This is stupid! We want to go home. If we weren't here in this awful place, this accident never would have happened." They could have complained loud and long about their supervisors, their companions, and their horrible accommodations. The could have said, "This has been the worst experience of our lives."

Wendy's team didn't choose to do those things. Rather they knelt in prayer, praying over and over into the night. Finally, at 3:00 A.M., the team received a call on the shortwave radio saying that their friend would be okay. In fact, not one bone in the girl's hand had been broken.

Wendy says, "That's when I cried, not because of my troubles and problems, but out of gratitude." Yes, her tears were an expression not of self-pity but of appreciation. Wendy felt as if she had truly witnessed a miracle!

These pictures tell the story of what happened in New Guinea. The one on the left shows the bridge that Wendy and her team built. The one on the right shows that a different kind of building was going on. That growth shows in Wendy's countenance as you can feel the love she developed for the people she was serving.

When my daughter finally came home, I was waiting as she got off the plane. She looked like a native. She had on a long muumuu and was carrying spears. She was tanned and exhausted, smiling and laughing. Handing her spears to one of her teammates and signaling for me to wait, she whipped off her muumuu. Underneath she had on a nice skirt and top that she had bought in Australia. She looked fantastic. She was healthy and in shape, felt great, and had a big smile on her face.

I asked her what she wanted to do first. "I want to take a real bath," she said with feeling. When we got home and Wendy turned on the water, she stared at it as if hypnotized. "Look, Mom, running water out of a tap!"

In the days that followed, *Wendy couldn't stop counting her blessings.* Suddenly she was seeing all the good things in her life. She had gained a testimony that God lives, loves us, and really is there for us.

At the start of her senior year, Wendy went to the same hairdresser we had visited the previous year. After the cut, Wendy looked in the mirror and said, "I love it. I just love it, and I love you, too!" The hairdresser almost fainted.

My daughter had a wonderful senior year. The teachers were the same as the year before. The students were the same. The school had not changed. But—and here's the point—Wendy's attitude had.

There are many things in your life that you cannot change. There are a lot of things about your body that are beyond your control. But there is one *big* thing that you have total and complete control over: your attitude. A very wise man, John Milton, said, *"The mind is its own place, and in itself can make a heav'n of hell, a hell of heav'n."*

Keep looking for the good things in your life. A great attitude will bring you a great life. Stay happy.

Love, Barbara

P.S. Abraham Lincoln said, "Happiness is a state of mind; we are as happy as we make up our minds to be." When it comes to your attitude, your mind is such a powerful tool because *your mind believes what you tell it, whether it's true or not.*

I went to a seminar in which the teacher called a volunteer to the front of the class and asked for her to stick her right arm straight out in front of her. The teacher would then try to push the girl's arm back down to her side. The volunteer was fairly strong, but with two hands, the instructor didn't have much trouble pushing the arm down.

Next, she told the volunteer to say five times and mean it, "I feel tired and weak." The volunteer did as instructed. Again she extended her arm. This time the teacher easily lowered the volunteer's weakened arm.

Finally, the teacher said, "Say five times, 'I feel great and strong,' and really mean it." With exuberance and power in her voice and a smile on her face, the volunteer did her part. When the instructor told her to stick out her arm once again, there was such strength in it that, try as she may, the teacher could not budge it.

Each day you have the power to tell your mind good and positive things or negative, critical, and ugly things. And your mind will believe you! If you spend your time, like my daughter Wendy did, in looking for the worst year, month, or day in your life, believe me, you will find it. Life is a self-fulfilling prophecy.

Here's your assignment: Make a deal with yourself that for the rest of this day, until you go to bed, you will say only good, happy, positive, and uplifting things about yourself and everyone you come in contact with—your friends, your family, everyone. Dwell on the things that are fine and lovely. Think of all the things that you can praise God for and be glad about (see Philippians 4:8). See what it does for your attitude!

Chapter 5

With God Nothing Is Impossible

You've seen those old cartoons with a character who has an angel sitting on one shoulder and a devil on the other. Your life is kind of like that. The devil is always tearing you down, telling you every negative thing about yourself. He whispers, "You have no friends. You're not smart. God doesn't even hear your prayers." That little devil tells you that those negative things are true. You start going down, down, believing the deceptive words of doubt and discouragement. That little devil is sending out invitations to your own personal pity party.

The little angel on your other shoulder, all dressed in white, is telling you good things that are true. "You are pretty. You are smart. You are a wonderful friend. You are such a good person." That angel wants you to be happy with who you are and what you have.

The thing about happy people is that they make their own happiness. They "listen to the angel" and look for the good in life. They expect miracles every day, and miracles happen because they are watching for them. They know God hears their prayers, because they are praying to him constantly. They have a positive attitude.

This is a sad letter from a girl who has a lot of work to do on her attitude.

Dear Barbara,

I sit here now at rock bottom in the pitiful depths of depression. I hate absolutely everything about me. I don't even know where to begin. I feel so inadequate, inferior, so average. Jealousy has made me a depressed and hopeless person. I have unrealistic (I know they are unrealistic) goals to be the best at everything, yet I am so afraid of failing and not being best that I am not even the best at one thing because I don't even try anything!

I am just so average at everything. I will go through everything one at a time: I am average height. I am overweight. I make goals continually and fail every time I begin to start a program or try to change. My hair is a mess, permed, colored, no shine. It's nothing.

My eyebrows are each different. My eyelashes grow every direction. My nose is a "honker." My face is round and chubby, and my skin is splotched. My teeth are straight—however, they are very yellowish. My hands are short and stubby, my fingers fat and crooked. I guess I'm just an all-around failure.

Spiritually I am a mess, too. I love the gospel, but I have let everything slide—prayer, scriptures, tithing, everything. I can't be worthy of His help any more.

Thank you for listening to my self-pity (another fault), but I pray that you will write me back and let me know if you even saw this letter.

Thank you, Natalie

Dear Natalie,

As I read your letter, I thought of three girls that I wish you could meet. Any of those girls could have written a letter very similar to the one you wrote. Lisa could have said, "I am deaf, so I can't do a lot of things others do." Jana could have said, "I hate living my life in a wheelchair." Heather could say, "If only I had two arms and looked like other girls."

But, Natalie, if you met these girls you would be so inspired. I know you would have to say, "If Lisa, Jana, and Heather can do it, then *so can I!*" Let me tell you about each one of them.

Lisa Jolley was selected as Miss Utah Teen. She won with her talent of piano performance. Now, thousands of people play the piano, but Lisa is deaf. She has never been able to hear the notes she plays. When the music is loud enough, she can detect the vibration of the beat. That's all. And yet she dares to perform intricate classical piano pieces for large audiences.

Lisa said, "When I was a baby, at one and a half, I lost my hearing when I contracted spinal meningitis. When I was two, I started going to the Utah School for the Deaf. My mother always wanted

her daughter to do many things, like dancing and playing the piano, but she thought that because of my hearing impairment there was no way that I would be able to do those things.

"One day when my mother was talking to the principal, she told him of her dilemma. He told her, 'Never suppose the limitations of a handicapped child.' From then on my mother put me into dancing at the age of four, gymnastics at five, and piano at seven.

"There was a time when I got so sick of being pushed to practice the piano all the time that I seriously thought about quitting. My mother sat down and talked to me. She said that I pleased my Heavenly Father when I played. I thought about it for a while, and I decided to stay at the piano even though it would mean a lot of practicing. I felt it would be something I could share with others.

"Remember what my principal told my mother, 'Never suppose limitations.' That statement does not apply only to a handicapped person but to everyone. There are many times we put limits on ourselves. The most important thing is to have a positive attitude and to never, ever give up.

"There have been times when I have wondered, Why am I deaf? Why me? I began to understand when I got my patriarchal blessing at age fifteen. It said that being deaf was part of my mission in life. Through it I would bring happiness through service and example to hundreds and hundreds of people in my life. Our trials are not given to us to make our lives miserable. The purpose of trials is to help us become stronger and grow from them.

"Remember to be positive and to never suppose your limitations and know that Heavenly Father has a fantastic plan for your life." Lisa is now serving a mission.

Another girl I want to tell you about is Jana Stump, Kansas Junior Miss. She competed and won in a wheelchair. She had a smile that literally lit up the stage. And you should have seen her wheelchair dance! She is also an incredible athlete and played basketball with Team USA in Atlanta for the Paralympics, in which 121 nations competed.

Jana was the passenger in a car involved in an automobile accident. Her friend lost control of the vehicle while driving over some rough railroad tracks. They hit the side of  an embankment. It could have been a minor accident, except that the seat Jana was sitting in broke and so did Jana's back, paralyzing her from the waist down. She says she is lucky to have complete control of her arms, hands, lungs, and brain.

After the accident, although confined to a wheelchair, she learned to become completely self-sufficient. Before the accident, Jana had been a competitive baton twirler. After her accident, she was a cheerleader. Jana says, "When the other girls were doing cartwheels and back flips, I smiled and popped my wheelies. At the girls' basketball games, instead of running up and down the court, I smiled and played the keyboard in the pep band. In my dance choir, the instructor added an extra girl singer so that everyone would have a partner. I just did the actions with myself, not having to worry about stepping on anyone's toes. I was still involved, just in different ways." But still Jana didn't feel like she had much self-esteem.

Jana entered the Junior Miss program. She knew people were wondering how she was going to pull it off. "Every aspect of the program was positive," Jana said. "It was not only a great experience for me but it also made others aware. Even though I steer a wheelchair, I'm still the same person. I don't feel that I won the program because people felt sorry for me; I felt that I actually deserved the title. And that's when I feel I regained my self-confidence."

Finally, I'd like to introduce you to my good friend Heather Barker. She competed in a Miss USA State pageant and won the Spirit Award.

Heather was born with only one arm. I was so amazed by her. She was doing everything all the other girls were doing. She was

friendly and outgoing. She was so confident on stage. Just for a few minutes when they first met her, the other girls didn't quite know what to say or how to act, but Heather was always smiling, friendly, and so kind to them that they quickly relaxed around her.

Heather showed me how she does a lot of things. She blow-dries her hair by tucking her dryer under her arm and then brushing her hair out with her one hand. She can only put on her pantyhose by sitting on the floor and doing a version of a one-handed tug-of-war. And you should see how she puts on and takes off her pierced earrings. She's like a magician.

But the part that blows me away is Heather's attitude. She is so happy! I asked her to come with me to speak at a youth conference. With great confidence and with a gorgeous smile on her pretty face, she proceeded to tell all the youth in the audience: "I do not feel handicapped. I was born this way, and I've never known anything different."

She went on to tell them that she began to feel insecure when she was about eleven. She said that was when she decided that nothing was going to change, so why let it ruin her life? Now she has such a positive attitude that people just like to be around her. I told her, "Heather, wherever you are and whatever you are doing, you will always have friends."

You see, Natalie, nothing about their situation changed for these girls. What made the difference was their attitudes. I know it's hard to decide suddenly one day that you're going to be different, that you're going to feel better about yourself, but it needs to start with a positive attitude.

The only way you can change to be like Jana, Lisa, and Heather is with God's help. President Ezra Taft Benson said, "Apart from God we cannot succeed, but as a partner with God we cannot fail" (*The Teachings of Ezra Taft Benson* [Salt Lake City: Bookcraft, 1988], p. 413). Yes, we all have weaknesses and imperfections, but through the Lord's grace he will make weak things become strong (see Ether 12:27).

I know that you can do it. As you see things improve in your life, please write to me and let me know how you're doing.

Love, Barbara

P.S. I took a taxi to the airport the other day and was talking with the driver. He seemed remarkably happy and positive, with a huge smile. I asked, "What's your secret?"

He said, "After my wife died, it was hard for me to get through the days, especially the holidays. Then one day, I decided I was tired of always being down in the dumps, so I made a decision. From that day forward, I would celebrate only one holiday every single day of the year—Thanksgiving!"

I said, "Gosh, what a great attitude you have."

"Do you know where a Great Attitude comes from?" he responded. "Think of the abbreviation for Great, as in Great Britain.

It's GR. Now add that abbreviation to Attitude. GR + Attitude = Gratitude. That's where it comes from, being grateful every day for all that we have. That's celebrating Thanksgiving every day of our lives."

Here's a hint for getting started on your positive attitude. Put a rubber band on one of your fingers. Don't put it on too tight. Wear that rubber band to remind you to say only positive things for twenty-four hours. Make a little rule for yourself that you can't skip anyone. Make each person you see feel better. That includes the girl you see each morning in the mirror. Say nice things to her too.

Part 2

Love One Another

Dear Barbara,
I love my friends, but they're driving me crazy. And my parents don't understand me at all. What can I do?

Chapter 6

How to Make Friends

In an earlier chapter I invited you to think about the popular people you know. What makes people like to be around them? It seems they have found the secret to making and keeping friends. This secret is something you can learn too.

I received the following letter from a girl named Lisa. See if you can relate to some of the things she writes:

Dear Barbara,

Sometimes things go really great for me, but overall, I don't feel loved. I'm not very popular, either. I really only have one friend. Last year I ate lunch by myself because my friend had a different lunch time. I did the best I could to see if there was a group of people I'd like to be a part of, and there wasn't! I'm not ugly, so why don't I have any real friends?

I am what you call extremely shy. (I wish that I wasn't.) How can I overcome this problem? I don't know. I've always been a quiet person. I just don't feel comfortable around people, and I don't know what to say. I get scared, freeze up, and can't carry on a conversation. I can't even think straight. But I'm so lonely, and I want friends.

I have been taught the importance of obeying the counsel of the bishop. I had an interview with him recently, and I talked about this problem. He told me to attend all of the firesides and activities that I could to get involved and make friends. He also quoted the familiar saying, "To have a friend, you must be a friend." I want to be friendly, bubbly, and outgoing, and be the type of daughter Heavenly Father wants me to be, but I just don't know where to begin.

Sometimes I feel like I'm drowning. I guess that I'm hoping you will throw me a lifeline. I don't know how much longer I can handle this. I hope to hear from you soon.

Love, Lisa

Dear Lisa,

There is so much that goes into making friends, and your bishop was right that you have to be a friend if you want to have friends. But learning how to be a friend takes effort.

I want to share with you some secrets about how shyness can be changed into warmth and, more important, how caring about others with no thought of anything for yourself can cause miracles to happen in your life.

Before we talk about anything else, I need to explain a little bit about how our brains work. One expert, Bert Decker, has described it like this: We have what is called a *first brain*. This is the *primitive brain* that reacts like a newborn baby reacts. What happens when a stranger leans over the crib and says, "Gootchie, gootchie, goo!" The baby screams. The baby has no idea what this big, scary person making silly noises is doing. Then the mother goes over and says, "Do do do dooo." The baby smiles. The baby knows this nice mommy person, silly noises and all, by instinct.

Another example of how the primitive brain functions is similar to an animal's instinct. When you see a strange dog, maybe a big Doberman or a pit bull, coming right at you, you might feel scared. I certainly feel scared, because I was attacked by a collie when I was in the first grade. So when I see a big dog coming, the minute he gets near me, I'm sure he'll bite me. At least that's how I feel. That's how my first brain reacts.

A similar thing happens in reverse when a person is fearful about approaching a horse. We don't always know it, but the horse usually senses our fear. What happens? The horse neighs and tries to back away from us. Then we become more frightened—and it becomes even more skittish. It's going to be difficult to get horse and rider together.

The rattlesnake has an even more primitive brain. It will strike when it senses anyone or anything getting too close.

This instinct, or first impression, is strong and very difficult to overcome. And what we *see* as a first impression can have a bigger impact than what we *read* or *hear*. This is the part of the brain that will fight first and ask questions later. It is the part of the brain that knows within a few seconds if we want to get to know someone new. The first brain is the part of us that never grows up. It is childlike. We will always have the instincts of a child, wanting to be warm and

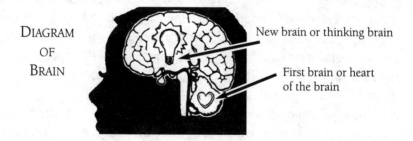

DIAGRAM
OF
BRAIN

New brain or thinking brain

First brain or heart
of the brain

secure. We want approval and trust and love. The first brain is what I call the heart of our brain.

This first brain, or the heart of the brain, has a *gatekeeper* leading into the much larger area of the brain where all our knowledge and memories are stored. All messages must pass through the heart of the brain, where first impressions are made. If that gatekeeper trusts and likes what it understands about us, then the second brain or thinking brain can open to us, and most likely we can become friends. (The above information was paraphrased from *High Impact*

Communication, a set of 12 audiocassettes by Bert Decker [Niles, Ill.: Nightingale Conant, n.d.].)

Your Circle of Influence

I once met a young woman named Lee Ann who was very bright and poised, but seemed to lack warmth. She had won the crown in the Miss Tennessee USA pageant, but I wondered in the back of my mind if she had the inner warmth that it takes to win the Miss USA crown.

Lee Ann came to train with me. When I met her at the airport as she stepped off the plane, she seemed so different! She was glowing, smiling, and absolutely effervescent. I had to ask, "What happened to you? You seem different! You're so much more confident, outgoing, warm, and friendly." I was anxious to know her secret so I could pass it on.

Lee Ann told me that a teacher had advised her: "Imagine a big circle around yourself, a circle about ten feet in diameter. This circle accompanies you as you walk. This is *your* space. It belongs to you, but it's up to you to make every person who comes into your space, your circle, feel really good about himself or herself."

"So," Lee Ann explained, "now when anyone steps into my *circle of influence,* I feel that, since I am in charge of this space, I need to smile and speak to that person. I need to make each one feel important and special."

Imagine what would happen if you walked down the hall of your school with a big, warm, real smile on your face. Anyone who steps into your circle, you look right into that person's eyes and say, "Hi." The heart of the brain would have a great first impression, which might start to open the gateway. And often, if you make people laugh, the gate will be wide open. Now the opportunity is there to talk and learn about each other and explore the idea of being friends.

Another tricky thing about the *circle of influence* method is that you tend to get back exactly what you give. I tried this one day when I was out walking. For every person I passed, I smiled differently. For one man, I smiled a big smile and said, "Hi, how are you today?"

He smiled back with an equally big smile and said, "Oh, fine!" Then I gave a women a moderate smile. I smiled and just said "Hi." I got back exactly what I gave out.

If you're shy, you're probably always looking down around other people, avoiding their eyes, waiting for them to make the first move. Chances are, they will respond with the same actions. Their actions aren't from shyness—they are just giving back exactly what was given to them! To change this, all you need to do is start smiling (a warm, *real* smile). You'll be surprised what just doing that one thing does to improve your friend-making ability.

Fake It until You Make It

Many people consider themselves shy. When they have to make the first move in meeting a new person, their hearts beat fast, their brains seem to quit working, and they break out in a cold sweat. Incredibly, you *can* learn to overcome much of your shyness.

You've heard the old saying, "Fake it until you make it." In other words, smile and say hello to people, even if you are afraid. Practice looking people in the eye when you speak to them. Pretend that you're not shy. You're the only one who will know you're faking it, and eventually you'll become better and better at it until you really won't be faking it anymore.

Sometimes people mistake shyness for being conceited. Another girl wrote me a letter telling me what happened to her in high school:

Dear Barbara,

When I was in high school, I was so shy that I didn't say hi to people at school. My junior year I decided to change because some boys my age told me I was too conceited to speak to anyone. What a shock! Anyway, I worked at being outgoing, and by my senior year I was Homecoming Queen and voted most popular girl.

Now, it is unusual for such a big change to take place in such a short time. But even if this girl had made only one new friend, or had just become more comfortable with the people she knew, it would still have been worth the effort.

Think of Others

One of the best ways to overcome shyness is to forget yourself

and concentrate on others. I know you've heard that before, but before you feel like I'm just saying empty words, let me give you some examples.

I met in Australia an incredibly kind woman named Margaret Morrison. She really did not have much money, but each Christmas, and sometimes during the year, she would dress up as Santa Claus and buy little trinket gifts for hundreds of children out of her meager income. Her kindness made a lasting impression on me. Margaret is one of my all-time heroines.

Another incredible woman is Elaine Clough, also from Australia. She heard I was in the hospital. She wrote me the most delightful note, saying she was thinking of me and wishing she could afford to send flowers from such a distance. Instead, she sent me a photo of some beautiful flowers. I

was touched beyond words by her thoughtfulness. I will never forget her or that special photograph.

Erica Havig, Miss Montana 1992, while at the Miss America pageant was invited along with some other contestants to go to a famous designer's salon to try on some evening gowns. She was so excited and so appreciative that she wrote the designer a thank-you note. Later he responded, saying that no one had ever written a thank-you note to him for trying on his gowns. He was so impressed that he offered to let her pick out and wear one of his gowns for her competition.

What Can You Do?

Think of other people. Get in the habit of writing thank-you notes—to your teachers (especially that one teacher you're really not "fond" of), to adults who do favors for you, to friends who are particularly kind. Just looking for chances to send thank-you notes will make a difference in your life. Always be watching for the good things people do. When you start looking for and acknowledging the good around you, it will make you happy. When you're happy, it is easier to be outgoing and friendly. And I can guarantee that you'll make loads of new friends.

By the way, you said you have one good friend. Be sure to pay attention to that friend. As you are getting to know new people, don't be so unkind as to start excluding your friend. Be the kind of person you want to become.

Don't make up your mind too quickly about who you would like to be friends with and who you wouldn't. Sometimes the people who become our best friends turn out to be a surprise.

Make a plan. For example, for a whole week, when you sit down in class, say hello to the person sitting behind you. That's all you have to do. Just say hi. It would be nice if you added the person's name, but you don't have to. They may even be surprised that you said hi, because you haven't been doing it. Say hi every day, and they'll start to expect it. Be patient. Things may not change too quickly. Give it lots and lots of time.

During the second week, go up and tell your Young Women advisor that you enjoyed the lesson. Look into her eyes when you say it, smile, and talk loudly enough for her to hear.

During the third week, *keep saying hi* to the people sitting around you in class, and start watching the people at school for things that they do especially well. For example, if you went to the school play and saw that someone you know had one of the parts or was in the chorus or orchestra, just tell them that you thought the play was good and that you saw them in it. You don't have to think of a whole bunch of things to say. One sentence is a great start.

The hard part is that everyone at school is used to you not talking or smiling. So you may feel like you are interrupting them. They may even be talking to other friends and not stop talking when you walk up. It's okay. Just say, "Excuse me. I heard you won your debate match. Congratulations." They'll probably say thanks. You can just leave then, but next time you walk up to them, they'll know you're going to say something and will pay attention.

I know this sounds hard, but *give yourself little assignments* each week and do them. You'll gradually see things start to change for the better. Lots of people want to be nice to you, but sometimes they don't know how to do it.

As you begin to become a little bit comfortable around someone, don't always hang back. After you say hi to them while they are with their friends, don't be too quick to walk away. If it feels comfortable, just keep standing with them as they talk. Teenagers don't always know how to make other people feel included, so if you just walk away, they'll think you left because you wanted to. Or maybe, like the girl who wrote the letter, they'll think you are conceited instead of shy.

There is one more terribly important thing that you need to know as you work at overcoming your shyness. You have one friend who will always be with you and love you. It is your Heavenly Father.

God has promised to help you in every good thing you want in your life. Turn to him. When you pray, tell him of your plans and ask him to help you feel calm and comfortable. He will help you in ways that will surprise you. When you feel his love for you, it will give you confidence. Tell him how much you would like to have a friend, and ask him to help you know the things you need to do to become the kind of friend others will want to have.

I know you can do it. Believe it. Try some of these suggestions. Will you promise me that you'll try the things we've talked about every day for one month? Stay happy.

Love, Barbara

P.S. Remember these friendly tips:

1. Write tons of thank-you notes.

2. When someone calls on the phone, make that person glad *you* answered.

3. When you enter a room, always say hello to everyone there.

4. Be a good listener. Be truly interested in what others have to say.

5. Stand up straight and don't look at the ground when you walk.

6. Do nice, unexpected things for people.

7. Make a plan of what you will do the first week, the second week, and the third week. Make sure you include little daily assignments for yourself each week.

8. Above all, SMILE!

Chapter 7

If I Met Myself, Would I Want to Be Friends?

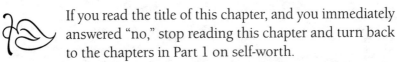 If you read the title of this chapter, and you immediately answered "no," stop reading this chapter and turn back to the chapters in Part 1 on self-worth.

First, you must believe that every person has something to give. Everyone is worth knowing. However, it is difficult to have dozens and dozens of equally close friends. It is more normal to have a small group of close friends, people who understand you and love you just the way you are. Then there are many other people who might be your close friends if it were possible for you to spend more time together. Finally, there are lots of people who you can enjoy being around in casual situations, but who will never become anything more than acquaintances.

If there is one thing that will help you develop a group of close, enjoyable friends, it is learning how to *be a friend*. In other words, if you met yourself, would you want to be friends?

Let me have you read parts of two letters I received.

Dear Barbara,

I think that I am the ugliest person. I don't have any self-esteem. My mom and dad say I am pretty, but I don't think I am. I think I'm fat, but people say I'm not. I'm not smart at all. Well, at least that's what I think. I want to go to BYU when I'm older, but I know I won't get in.

Please write back.

This is the second letter:

Dear Barbara,

I have a problem. Whenever I go to a church event, I get angry. Often someone says something that bugs me. I don't get angry at them. I get annoyed and then get angry at myself for letting it bother me. Other times I just get annoyed with how insane everything seems.

I haven't had an informative Sunday School lesson in years. I've heard all the stories in the books before. Our Young Women leaders gave us a three-month calendar of upcoming activities. Only about two sound enjoyable. The rest sound like a big waste of my time.

Youth conference was at the stake center. We sat for hours listening to people talk. Then we went to a hot gym at a college campus and were told to entertain ourselves for a few hours. Then we went to a park for a dance. I hate dances, and this one lasted about four hours.

We spent the night at a hotel, which must have been expensive, and I got stuck with the Beehives (I'm a Laurel). We had nothing in common.

Girls camp this year had zero spirituality, which is usually the best part of camp. Anyway, you see my problem? What should I do? I'm having a hard time getting the Spirit into my life, too. Probably because of all my negative feelings. I'm writing to you because if I said this aloud to anyone, I would have sobbed through the whole thing.

Thanks for taking the time to read this.

Just from reading these letters, do you think you would be friends with either of these girls? Why not?

You're all dressed, ready to go out the door, but you stop to check yourself in the mirror one last time. You look at your hair, your makeup, your clothes. Wait: here are a few more things you need to check before you walk out the door. You just can't see any of these in a mirror. Carefully read each item below and put a check mark beside the numbers of the items that describe the real you. Be honest!

A Negative Checklist

❏ 1. *Are you always looking for trouble?* Do you always see the glass as half empty, never half full? Are you always looking for problems or flaws? And do you always have to make sure that others know about those problems or flaws? For example, would you ever catch yourself saying, "The music was just awful," or "Do we always have to have cookies and punch for refreshments?" or "She didn't even say hi. She just thinks she's better than we are"?

❏ 2. *Are you sarcastic?* Are you always making jokes at someone else's expense? When you say hurtful things, do you excuse yourself with, "Just kidding"?

I remember a guy who looked at my feet and said, "Do you ski on those?" That hurt. I wasn't laughing. A joke isn't funny unless everyone can laugh. Sarcasm is the lowest form of humor.

❏ 3. *Are you a gossip?* Do you love to spread the latest story you've heard to all your friends? You might excuse yourself by saying, "This isn't gossip because it's true." But if it's hurtful, keep it to yourself!

❏ 4. *Are you jealous?* Let me tell you about some girls I knew. Amy was assigned to be lab partners with Chris. At first, Amy was pleased because Chris was so beautiful and popular. Then

Amy became jealous. She kept comparing all the things Chris had to her own shortcomings. Her jealousy made her depressed.

One day, Chris was not at school. Amy heard that her lab partner had tried to commit suicide! Amy was amazed. How could this have happened? Chris had everything. Why would she want to take her own life?

Amy went to see Chris in the hospital. Chris was so glad that Amy had come. None of her so-called "popular" friends had come to see her or even called. Chris poured out her heart to Amy, saying that she had always tried to look and act the way people wanted her to, and she didn't think anyone cared who she really was.

Amy and Chris grew to be friends, and Amy learned a valuable lesson. Things are not always as they appear, and everyone has his or her own set of problems. Learn to appreciate who you are and what you have.

❏ 5. *Are you possessive?* If you make friends, do you cling to those friends until they feel like they are suffocating? Do you get hurt and angry if your friends don't include you in absolutely everything? It is a natural instinct to pull away when someone is trying so hard to possess you.

❏ 6. *Are you thoughtless?* When you whisper about and exclude others, it is not only bad manners, it can be damaging, too. If a bunch of people are planning to go out for pizza, do you include everyone? Or do you say things like, "I don't like them. Let's get away from them." Being thoughtless of other people's feelings is insensitive and tactless.

❏ 7. *Are you conceited?* Do you have to constantly look at yourself?

I had a friend who was a ballet dancer. Whenever I was with her, she had to look at her reflection in every store window and mirror we would pass. She was always more interested in how she looked than who she was with or what they were saying. It was not very much fun to go anywhere with her.

❏ 8. *Do you just do the minimum required?* Do you take the easiest classes? If you're in a club or on a committee, do you always wait for someone else to volunteer for assignments? Do you just try to slide by, not doing your schoolwork?

❏ 9. *Are you insincere?* Do you always say the same supposedly nice thing day after day? "You look great today. I just love your outfit." After a few hundred times, no one believes you anymore. Compliments are wonderful, but they need to be sincere. Look for new things to say in a complimentary way.

❏ 10. *Do you hate to say you're sorry?* We all make mistakes, and accidents do happen. We need to admit them and be willing to apologize. Sometimes a verbal apology, "I'm sorry," is enough. But sometimes we need to do more. A sincere apology is a sign of maturity and allows us to put the matter behind us and continue being friends.

❏ 11. *Are you self-critical?* No one knows you better than you know yourself. If you could list all your good points and concentrate on them, your life would be so much better. Often we just keep rerunning a list of our faults and flaws and shortcomings, to the point that we become paralyzed by them.

When someone pays you a compliment, do you "correct" the person by pointing out what is really wrong with you? Learn to accept praise and compliments. Do your friends a favor and believe the nice things they say about you! And remember this: if you point out the bump on your nose (the one no one even noticed), it will be the only thing your friends will notice about you the next time they see you.

❏ 12. *Are you selfish?* Do you have to be first, get the most, or make sure that you get all the attention? Usually this happens at someone else's expense. Everyone wants a chance to be the star. People can blossom with attention, but when they demand attention, they become unappealing. If you demand attention—by having to dominate every conversation, for example—soon people will stop inviting you to join in, or they'll avoid being around you altogether.

❏ 13. *Do you have to have your own way?* It is not pleasant to be around people who have to have their own way all the time.

I heard about a missionary who had just arrived in the mission field. He accompanied his senior companion to carry out the plans he had already made with some other missionaries for preparation day. They were going to play volleyball. Suddenly, the senior companion looked around and couldn't see the new missionary. He and the others began to search. They finally found him at the home of a member, just visiting. He said that he hadn't wanted to play volleyball, so he had just taken off alone. He sent a clear message that he was quite accustomed to doing only what pleased him, showing a lack of concern for what others wanted to do or how his actions would affect them.

❏ 14. *Are you a poor loser?* After the game or competition is over, are you likely to say that it wasn't fair or that your loss was so-and-so's fault? You can't wish anyone well because you or your team didn't win. You can't accept defeat with style. Good losers always compliment the winners.

❏ 15. *Do you put people down?* I can remember a time when a friend I greatly admired began to criticize others. I would just sit and listen and smile. I was afraid that if I said anything, she wouldn't be my friend anymore. I didn't suspect she would talk about me to others. But she did, and it hurt me very deeply. I realize now that I should have known I would not be exempt. Don't choose friends who are critical of others. And remember, the people you care about should be able to depend on *you* to not talk behind their backs.

Now that you've finished reading this list, look carefully at the numbers you have checked. These are the things you need to work on. Take a little sticky note and write down the items you marked. Then put the sticky note on your mirror or by the phone to remind yourself of what *not to do!* You might even tell your friends what you're working on and get them to help you. There is strength in numbers.

Contrast those negative habits with the attitude of the young woman who wrote this letter:

Dear Barbara,

I have one shot at every day of my life, and I get them one at a time. I wake up in the morning and say to myself, "Am I going to be happy or sad?" Then I put a smile on my face and begin my day.

This girl has already seen some good changes in her life. She is taking charge of her attitude. And she is choosing to be happy. It works.

Let me know how your positive attitude helps you in your friendships!

Love, Barbara

P.S.: Don't forget to put the list of negative things that you checked off on a sticky note. In fact, make more than one, and put one on your mirror, one on the phone, and one on your notebook or in your locker. Then remember the message of this poem:

The Girl in the Glass

When you get what you want in your struggle for gain,
And the world makes you Queen for a Day,
Just go to the mirror and look at yourself
And see what that girl has to say.

It isn't your father or mother or friend
Whose judgment upon you must pass.
The one whose verdict counts most in your life
Is the one staring back in the glass.

She's the one you must satisfy beyond all the rest
For she's with you right up to the end,
And you know that you've passed your most difficult test
When the one staring back is your friend.

You may be the one who got a good break,

Then say I'm a wonderful gal,
But the one in the glass says you're only a fake
If you can't call that person your pal.

You may fool the world down your pathway of years
And get pats on the back as you pass,
But your final reward will be heartache and tears,
If you've cheated the girl in the glass.

—Author unknown

What Bad Friends Can Do

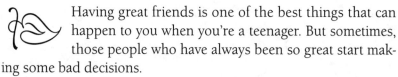 Having great friends is one of the best things that can happen to you when you're a teenager. But sometimes, those people who have always been so great start making some bad decisions.

It can tear you up inside because you like them so much. They are so cool to hang out with. You can talk about anything and everything. You can't imagine going through life without seeing them every day. And how will you survive school? They know just what to say to make you laugh like crazy.

But when they start making decisions to skip school, to drink, to smoke, to do drugs, to experiment with sex, you simply cannot do those things with them. You cannot save them from their bad decisions by going along with them. You will get sucked in, and then you will be just as lost as they are.

Let me have you read a letter from a girl who had trouble with her friends and their decisions:

Dear Barbara,

Three months ago I changed schools because my parents didn't like the direction that some of my friends were taking me.

At the beginning of the year, I loved school, my friends, and my life! My parents and I have never really gotten along. They have always disapproved of my friends because they look a little different and do "weird" things. They wouldn't let me go out with my friends anymore because they thought my friends would make me do some of the wild things they do. So they made me change schools.

It's been seriously hard trying to make new friends and trying to fit in. But I guess my parents were right. I had been doing some really bad things and hanging out with some guys that I shouldn't have. I've finally stopped seeing my boyfriend (I'm only fifteen), and it hasn't been easy. I think that I love him, and it's been hard living without him lately.

I'm not sure what to do. I feel like my life is a complete mess. Please advise me. I never thought this could happen to me, but I'm living proof that bad friends really can get you to do bad things.

Thanks, Bonnie

Dear Bonnie,

I have read so many letters from girls who start out with friends they think are so great, so much fun. But then bad things start happening.

One summer, when I visited girls camp, I met two of the cutest girls. They were juniors in high school and best friends. One year later, I received a letter from one of those girls. I want to share her story with you.

Dear Barbara,

My friendship with Megan began when I moved from Texas to Mesa, Arizona. Megan lived a few houses up, and we were soon inseparable. We had so much fun.

At the end of the eighth grade, Megan's family moved about twenty miles away, but she didn't change schools. Every day Megan and I would ride the bus to her house, and my dad would pick me up on his way home from work. We also spent the weekends together, going to the mall, having sleepovers, talking lots of girl talk, taking dance lessons, going to church, normal stuff. Then we started high school, and Megan had to change schools.

As high school went on, Megan started spending more and more time with Alison. Alison was into drugs. At the same time, Megan's home life was getting more challenging–her parents divorced and her three older brothers and her sister were on drugs and unhappy. Megan saw how hard it all was on her mom and told me, "I will never do that to my mom–never!"

Megan resisted Alison's relentless determination to get her high–until the end of her junior year. Megan decided that, since she was moving with her family to Las Vegas, Nevada, trying pot just once before she left wouldn't hurt. But it wasn't just once. Then, when she moved, she found a new group of friends. The friends got worse and the drugs got worse, more frequent and harder. She would go to school only when she felt like it, always thinking she could catch up. She didn't graduate from high school. She now lives with her boyfriend, who's going to be a tattoo artist. Her once beautiful blonde hair is in dreads, and her tongue is pierced. As the drugs get heavier, the light in her eyes gets darker and darker. She has closed me out of her life.

And all I remember her telling me is that her friends wouldn't influence her. Megan, my good friend, I still love you.

Can't you feel how much this girl misses her friend? She can't talk to her or visit her because Megan won't let her into her life. And all that happened in a little over a year. One wrong decision led to another and another. Now, in just this short time, Megan's life has become a real mess, and it will take years to undo all the damage, if she's even still capable of turning her life around.

How can her friend help? How can you help your friends who are starting to make really bad decisions in their lives?

There is only one way. You can't give in. You have to be a rock, someone stable they can return to when they want to come back. You may even have to stay away from them for a while. You can stay in touch and let them know you care, but, no matter how lonely it makes you, your decisions cannot be influenced by theirs.

Even though you love your friends dearly and would do anything in the world for them, you simply cannot go along with them on their downward slide. They will say things that will make you feel guilty. "So, now you think you're better than I am. Is that why you won't party with me?" "If you were a real friend, you wouldn't judge me." But the only way you can really help is by being the one who makes the right decisions.

You may even catch yourself worrying that you're being self-righteous, or proud of yourself, or stuck up. That's not it. You have to be strong in doing what you know is right. When you feel yourself getting weak, turn to the strongest people you know for help. Don't give up. Fight with everything you have to stay strong and choose the right. It's the only way you can ever help yourself or your friends.

If you go along with your friends just to try to protect them, to influence them to quit what they are doing, eventually you will get sucked in, and then both of you will be lost. It won't work. No one is strong enough to keep going to the wrong places and doing the wrong things over and over. Don't fool yourself by thinking that you will be the exception. You won't be.

I need to tell you another story about a girl I know. Let's call her Eva.

Eva was in the eighth grade when she began to slip. The slide she embarked on wasn't particularly steep at the start, but it was slippery, and as the ride continued, she picked up speed.

At first, Eva didn't worry about heading for trouble because it all seemed kind of fun. A new best friend, Francine, had come into her life. Francine very shortly came to mean the world to Eva. Eva had already pushed everyone else away, family included, but that seemed okay because she was busy with her friend. They messed around in class, talked back to their teachers, and slipped into their chairs after the tardy bell had rung. No biggie.

In the ninth grade, Francine casually broke the news to Eva that now she was doing drugs. Eva had known that her friend drank and was sexually active, but those things didn't seem to matter to their friendship. Francine bragged about her actions, and her reputation became worse and worse. It didn't matter to Eva what Francine did. She was her best and closest friend.

In fact, with nobody else to turn to, Eva started drinking and doing drugs with Francine. But not sex. Sex was where Eva drew the line.

Then, one horrible night, Eva was date-raped. She didn't even know the boy very well. He was just someone Francine partied with. That night, Eva lost her virginity, and that loss was horrible. The rape was not her fault, but looking back she knew she had been in the wrong place and was so drunk she was powerless to fight.

Eva had a boyfriend. He was hurt at first, but soon he decided that as long as Eva was no longer a virgin, they might as well have sex as well. And they did. What could Eva say?

A month or so after the rape, Eva was terrified that she might be pregnant. She didn't even know by whom. How could she know? After some awful days of waiting, she found out she wasn't pregnant after all.

The whole experience was a nightmare. She tried to break off with her boyfriend, but they kept drifting back together. Her life wasn't going anywhere. Miserable, she decided that life wasn't worth living.

First, Eva tried to slash her wrists. Then she tried overdosing on a combination of drugs, alcohol, and LSD. Nothing worked. Apparently, for some reason she was unable to understand, this was not the time for her to die.

The final week of the school semester arrived, and with it came that bitter, last straw. After all she had given him, her boyfriend decided he liked another girl better. He dumped Eva. Her reaction was to pick a fight with her mother and run away from home.

Eva moved in with Francine, and things went from horrible to worse. Francine was a monster who got Eva into things that are too horrifying to even write on paper.

Finally, Eva ran back to the people who really and truly loved her no matter what. At least, she hoped they still did. She prayed with all the strength she possessed that she had not killed their love. Her family welcomed her with open arms and tears of joy that their prayers had finally been answered.

But that wasn't the end. Eva found out she was pregnant. She went to her bishop, expecting to be condemned. Instead, she found someone who was willing to help her find the path back. Eva loved her baby enough to know that she had very little to offer the child. She decided to put her baby up for adoption, choosing to make something good and responsible out of the situation.

Eva discovered, too late, that good and righteous choices do not tie you down, as she had thought. These choices are the ones that make your life free and happy.

Hold Tight to the Iron Rod

The hard thing in friendships is being able to see those first baby steps in the wrong direction and stop before the situation becomes too serious. I wish that I could end here with a photograph, but since I can't I'll paint you a word picture:

Imagine that you're walking with your friend in a beautiful meadow of grass and wild flowers. The breeze is blowing your hair and your beautiful long dress, and it seems as if the air is filled with perfume. You look over at your friend. She is so happy, and you feel so grateful that such a great person likes you and likes doing the same things you do.

You are walking along beside the iron rod. It is sturdy and safe. Your parents and teachers have told you to walk beside it always and never take your hand off it.

But it's such a beautiful day, and the whole idea of there being something dangerous around seems ridiculous. Your friend yells, "Look, I'm going to run down this little hill to the river."

You're scared. You've been told never to go out of arm's reach of the rod. You yell back, "Don't. It's dangerous. Don't go that far."

But your friend laughs at you a little: "Oh, you're such a worrywart. Look around. Nothing can happen. We can come back to the rod anytime we want. It'll be fun. Come on."

She keeps working on you, "Don't be such a scaredy-cat. Are you always going to do everything your parents tell you? You're old enough to make up your own mind."

She takes off running down the hill. It looks like so much fun. She looks so free. But still, you can't go. You grab onto the rod until your knuckles turn white. Your friend even runs back up the hill and grabs the rod again herself. "See, it didn't hurt me one bit. And it was so interesting down by the river. You've just got to try it."

You're tempted. After all, she made it back to the rod with nothing bad happening. Again, your friend takes off down the hill. For a moment, you let go of the rod and take a step or two after her. Again you stop. You can't go against all those words of advice your parents and leaders have given you. But you watch your friend with envy. She gets to have all this fun, and you're stuck holding onto this stupid iron rod, and it just isn't very exciting.

Your friend stays longer and longer down by the river. Now her beautiful dress is getting torn and dirty. Her feet sink in the mud and gook. She loses her shoes. She's starting to cry. "Help! Come and help me. You're my best friend. Won't you come and be the strong one and help me through this?"

There are other people stuck in the mud as well. Some are even in the water of the river, desperately swimming for their lives. These people call to your friend, "Oh, you're okay. Don't look back up the hill toward the iron rod for help. That's only for children and those goody-goodys who don't know what life is really like."

Instantly, you know you can't leave the rod. If you go to your friend, you'll get stuck just as badly as she is. Then both of you will be wallowing in the mud. You could even get sucked into the whirlpools of the filthy water in the river. The voices of the others are getting louder. They are calling to your friend to give up and just sink into the waters of the river.

You can't bear it. You can't stand to lose your best friend. You decide to let go of the iron rod and run as fast as you can to your friend and help her back up the hill. Just as you decide to let go, you look at your family. Some are holding onto the iron rod. They are reaching out as far as they can stretch to other members of your family and helping them back so they can hold to the rod again. You see your mother's tears as she leans out but can't quite reach the fingertips of your older brother.

"Mom," you call. "I have to go help my friend. I just have to."

Your mother cries out, "No, please. Don't let go. It doesn't work. Believe me. I have seen it too often. Call to your friend. Have her pull herself up the hill as far as her strength will carry her. Then you can reach out to her and grab her hand and help her back to the iron rod. It's the only way."

You call to your friend as loudly as you can. She can barely hear your voice over the voices of the people caught in the filthy water. You yell to her, "Come back. It's your decision. If you come as far as you have strength, I'll reach out and pull you in the rest of the way."

Your friend struggles with everything she has to climb the hill. The thorns grab at her clothes, and the mud seems to be holding her feet. People by the river don't like to see her trying to get away. They keep grabbing at her arms to keep her with them. All the time, you're calling to her and encouraging her. She seems to be listening and is following your voice.

Finally, she struggles up the hill and collapses just a short distance from you. But it's close enough. You never let go of the rod, but you reach out with all your might. You're just able to grab your friend's hand. Gradually, she moves closer and closer to the rod until she can grab hold by herself. She bursts into tears and turns to you. "Thank you. Thank you so much. You've saved my life. I'll be forever grateful to you, my true friend."

You know what the iron rod is in this story. The scriptures describe it as the word of God (see 1 Nephi 11:25). Where do you find the word of God? In the scriptures, in prayer, and in the righteous teachings of your parents and Church leaders. Staying close to the iron rod, then, means staying on a righteous course.

Remember, you always have one perfect friend, someone who will never leave you and who always cares about you. That friend is Jesus Christ. With him, you can overcome anything.

Love, Barbara

P.S. Answer these two questions honestly, with no excuses.

1. Does my friend make it easier or harder to do the things I know I should?

2. Am I a better person when I am with my friend?

The rest is up to you . . .

Be a Builder,
Not a Wrecker

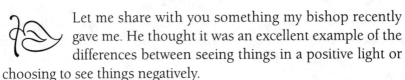 Let me share with you something my bishop recently gave me. He thought it was an excellent example of the differences between seeing things in a positive light or choosing to see things negatively.

First, he handed me a sheet of paper with two lists on it and a word mostly spelled out. He said, "Read each list, and then fill in the blank."

1. Apple	1. Sex
2. Orange	2. X-rated
3. Pear	3. Pornography
4. Peach	4. Violence
Fill in the blank: R__PE	Fill in the blank: R__PE

If you're like most people, you completed the word after the first list to say *ripe,* and the one after the second list to say *rape.* "You see," he said, "Your response depends on which list you read."

In other words, how can you have a good outlook or a positive attitude when the things you are surrounded by are negative or violent? That's why the language you use and the things you see and talk about are so important. They can color your whole outlook.

Sometimes your friends may accuse you of being a goody-goody because you refuse to listen to dirty jokes, use bad language, or go to R-rated movies. The more you are exposed to bad language, horrible images, awful music lyrics, or violent movies, the more you tend to see things based on those images.

An old Indian chief told a friend of mine, Laura Herring, "All of our lives, we have competing in us a black dog and a white dog."

"How do we know," asked Laura, "which one is winning?"

He answered, "By the one you feed the most."

How you feel depends on which dog, the white (positive) or the black (negative), you are feeding. Here's a letter from a girl who was hurt by the negative behavior of her friends:

Dear Barbara,

It was about February when one of my friends all of a sudden stopped talking to me. She didn't even want to be around me. She started spreading rumors about me that were not true at all. She got my other friends to hate me too. It was even worse because she was part of the popular group, so they joined in. They called me "wanna-be."

Every day when I get home, I cry and ask my Heavenly Father why this is happening to me. What should I do? Please help me!

Love, Julie

Dear Julie,

Have you ever put on a pair of glasses with colored lenses? For instance, those yellow-tinted glasses that snow skiers wear make the bumps and changes show up on a slope that otherwise would look flat and white. Suddenly everything looks different, more interesting, and often more beautiful.

Have you ever heard of looking at the world through rose-colored glasses? Everything looks rosy and warm. People use that phrase to describe a person who sees the good in everything.

Wouldn't it be nice to look at the world through Jesus-colored glasses? If you could look at the world through Jesus-colored glasses (let's called them "Son glasses"), you would be a builder and a light just like Christ wanted us to be for each other. But if you looked at the world through Satan-colored glasses, you would view the world the way he does, being negative, critical, judgmental, and gossipy.

Kenneth Cope wrote a song called "Backwords." No, that is not misspelled. *Backwords* means the damaging words spoken behind someone's back. The lyrics to his song go like this:

> Whether carefully begun to scar a name,
> Or recklessly continued without shame,
> Self-approval is the underlying plan.
> Fueled until the fire gets out of hand,
> Catastrophe—crippling words behind the scenes,
> Heartless talk that steals tomorrow's dreams.
>
> Chorus
> Who's gonna stop it? Who can,
> Once it gets started spreading, threatening.
> Has love become lost in the back words path?
>
> Now we pray for peace to keep us from the sword.
> Then we turn and wound a brother with a word.
> It's tragedy—blind to hypocrisy.
> We're wanting love when we're love's enemy.
>
> This road we take leads us to a bitter fate,
> Where judgement's terror stares us in the face.
> Who's gonna stop it, who then,
> When justice gets started and we're not ready?
> Regretting forever back words.
>
> Chorus
> Who's gonna stop it? We can!
> It's now or never.
> Let's change forever,
> And welcome love back to the forwards path.

From Voices (Nashville, Tenn.: Lightwave Records, 1991). Used by permission.

How many times do we hear gossip and allow it to continue on because we love secrets? But secrets can become rumors, which in turn become gossip. Wrong assumptions can spread and be used by Satan to wreck people's lives.

Stephen Covey, a nationally famous speaker and writer, tells of the time he got on a subway in a large city. There was a man in the same car with four little boys who were acting wild. They were disrupting the whole subway car, running up and down the aisles. Stephen Covey finally could stand it no longer. He approached the man and said: "Sir, pardon me, but I want you to know your children are disturbing everyone. Can't you control your children? Isn't there anything you can do?"

The man looked up at him sadly and said: "I'm sorry. I just came from the hospital where their mother died. I just don't quite know what to say to them right now. They've had such a shock. I don't want to be too strict. I'm sorry."

Brother Covey said that all of a sudden he felt very small. He had been looking at the situation through wrong-colored glasses. If he had had "Son glasses" on, he would not have said anything. His thought would more likely have been, *I wonder what is wrong with that man. I wonder if there is anything I could do to help him.*

We choose to look at life through our own glasses. Which ones do you use? Try to be a light instead of judging. Instead of criticizing, look for the good. See what you can do to help the situation. I'm sure you've heard your mother say, "If you can't say something nice, don't say anything at all." It's good advice. Build others up and make them feel good about themselves. Be helpful in a situation, and you will end up being the true winner.

Here are some specific examples of people who have learned to see only the negative side of a situation:

Example 1: In one high school there was a busybody girl who was always causing problems, always saying negative things, always gossiping. One day she could not wait to tell the entire school that she had seen the most popular boy and girl coming out of a motel at midnight. She said, "Well, I actually didn't see them, but my mom and dad were coming home from a party and saw them coming out of the motel."

You know how it is when someone tells you something like that.

The gossip–the wrecking–begins. The truth was that they had gone to the motel to use the phone in the lobby because they had car trouble.

Example 2: Once, in a doctor's waiting room, a girl who was wearing her Satan-colored glasses saw this nerdy guy from her school come out of the examination room. The girl heard the nurse say the report was back, and it was HIV-positive. She spread the gossip, and things became so hard for that boy and his family that they had to move. The truth was that the report mentioned by the nurse was regarding another patient. The girl had jumped to the wrong conclusion and wrecked some fine people's lives. (Even if the news had been true, however, it was not her place to spread it around.)

Example 3: A high school music teacher, in order to help his students keep the correct rhythm while playing their instruments, had the habit of tapping out the beat on his students' legs. He was accused by one of his young students and her parents of touching her inappropriately. He lost his job, suffered a mental breakdown, and had to cope with bouts of depression. Before his lawsuit finally came to trial, the girl and her parents retracted their complaint and said that she had not been improperly touched. But it was too late. He asked, "How can you recover from years of devastation?"

Example 4: What if the thing you want to tell others is true? That's certainly not gossip, is it? Before you decide, take a look at this letter:

> *Dear Barbara,*
>
> *I need some advice. I hope you can help me. A few weeks ago, a group of girls in my ward spread some rumors about me. The only problem is that these rumors are almost all the way true, but with some exaggeration. Their "rumors" deal with a guy in my ward that I like. They embarrassed him in front of everyone, and they really embarrassed me too.*
>
> *I hate going to church now. I've tried to talk to them, but they say I'm stuck-up, and they believe they've done nothing wrong. I NEED HELP! I know that I am not supposed to worry about what other people say, but I just can't get over this. I've even talked to my parents and Young Women leaders. It doesn't*

help. I've almost left my ward for another one. Is this wrong? What should I do?

Love, Marnie

Because of gossip, even about something that was true, this girl may end up changing wards—or worse, she may not go back to church. Of all places, church is where everyone should always feel welcome and loved.

The bottom line: if something you want to talk about or tell others is true but it is also hurtful and unnecessary, keep it to yourself.

I read a book written by a woman who had a near-death experience. I'm not sure I believe all that was in the book, but one part made me think. She said that when she died and went on to the next life, she was allowed to look back at the world. As she looked, she saw that many people were surrounded by a black light or aura. Other people had a white light or aura. She said a person with the black aura gave out bad things, and in return received back bad things. The person with a white aura gave out good and got back good. The more goodness they gave, the more goodness they received. Their light was beautiful, bright, and uplifting.

Isn't that how you want to be: a person with a white aura, a beautiful white light, surrounding you? Don't be a judge. Don't be a gossip. Don't spread rumors or make cutting remarks about others.

I once received a copy of an English essay that a high school girl had written. My heart broke when I read how lonely and isolated she felt. Then she wrote how she turned to the one friend who is always there, Jesus Christ, and how it literally saved her life.

Amber wrote about how many rude and unkind things people had said to her over the years. "The reason for my lost self-esteem," she wrote, "is that I have been made fun of all my life. At school, peers would say, 'Oh, here comes thunder thighs,' or 'Fat Albert's wife is coming.' These things hurt me deeply. I have never had a best friend or a really close friend. I normally had lunch by myself and did nothing on the weekends. I was nearly always by myself.

"The final straw was when my own family started making rude comments. My brothers and sisters and father would say, 'Don't you care about yourself?' But the most hurtful thing of all was when my mother said, 'Because of the way you look and the way you act, you will never have a boyfriend or get married.' I went to school that day and cried for two hours in the health office. I then decided that there was no purpose to my life since I had no one to talk to about the way I felt. I decided to take my life."

Amber then attended a young women's camp at BYU called "A Look At You." We talked a lot about letting the inner beauty each person has show on the outside. Amber said, "Learn to depend on the Lord by studying the scriptures, pondering, fasting, and praying. When I did this, it brought me a new best friend, one who would never hurt me—Jesus Christ. I realized that I have a special mission to complete on this earth. I found someone who loves me."

With the confidence this realization gave her, Amber talked with her family. "I forgave my mother and everyone who had hurt me in the past. I now have family and friends who accept me for who I am."

Amber concluded, "I know if people would not judge so harshly, and especially if they did not use words to wound each other, the world would be so much better."

All your life you will meet people with that "black aura." They will be negative and try to suck you into that negativity. You can be different. You can be a light, not a judge; build people up and make them feel good about themselves. Wear your "Son glasses."

Build Someone Every Day

My mom was the most incredible example I've ever known of a "people builder." When I was fourteen, my mother was a volunteer in a hospital. I was shocked when she decided one day that she was going to make certain patients "Hospital Queen for a Day." She made a glittery paper crown, a banner out of some white ribbon, and a poster that said "Hospital Queen." She created a bouquet out of some artificial roses she had in the garage. To top it all off, she told me that I was her official photographer. How embarrassing! We'd walk into the room of somebody we didn't even know and

make the presentation. I had to go
with my mother and watch this
scenario every week.

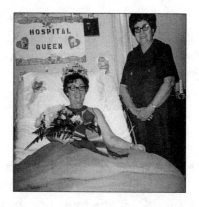

I was humiliated. I thought it
was the dumbest thing. Then, one
day, I overheard a woman talking
on the pay phone. She was saying:
"You'll never believe this. Mother
was chosen hospital queen. Out of
all the people in this hospital, she
was chosen the queen! She had a
crown, a banner, and a bouquet of roses. We even have a picture of
it. Yes, I'll send you a copy. I'll make thirty copies to send to all the
family and her friends."

My mother did that kind of thing her entire life. She would see
someone's picture in the newspaper, cut it out, glue it on a piece of
paper, decorate it with flowers, write congratulations, and send it to
the person. Today she's in a rest home suffering from Alzheimer's.
But just the other day, a lady told me that my mother had given her
an award on a scrap of paper in tiny, almost-impossible-to-read
handwriting. Even when there is hardly anything left of her, she is
still a builder.

My father, Neal J. Harrell, had a wonderful saying I'll always
remember: When you light a glow in someone else's heart, you feel
the warmth in your own.

I want to be like that, don't you? Everywhere you go, build
people up. Tell a young girl she has beautiful eyes. Tell your dad he's
wonderful. Write five thank-you notes every Sunday. Look for the
good in every person and every situation. And while you're looking
for the good in others, it will be coming back to you in waves.

When Christ was teaching his disciples, he told them that
the greatest commandment was to love their Lord and God. The
second commandment, which is really related to the first, is
"love one another; as I have loved you" (John 13:34). If you see
through "Son glasses," you can change the world for others. Be the
one to lead, and watch how others will follow. Let your white light
be contagious.

I know that God lives. I know that Jesus is the Christ. I know there is power in his name. Call upon him and look to his light to guide you along the journey back home.

Love, Barbara

P.S. When others start gossiping, there are a few things you can do.

1. *Change the subject.* Reporters and talk-show hosts are masters of turning the course of a conversation. Just watch as they guide a guest from one topic to another. You can do this too: "You know, before I forget, I want to ask you . . ." Or say, "Oh, sorry to interrupt, but before I forget, I just have to tell you about . . ."

2. *Walk away.* Make an excuse that you have to use the phone, or go to the bathroom, or get something to eat.

3. *Make a promise to yourself, then say, stop.* Make a promise to yourself that you are *not* going to participate in gossiping. Write it in your journal. Put a sticky note by the phone and on your notebook. You have a right to choose what you hear. Then, when gossip starts, say, "Please don't tell me. I've made a promise with myself that I'm trying not to gossip."

4. *Build others.* Point out the good things you've noticed in others before anyone can say something bad.

Chapter 10

My Parents Are Driving Me Crazy!

Does it sometimes seem like your parents were put on earth just to make your life miserable? I know how that can feel. But I also know that being a mom is hard. We want such good things for our children that we sometimes handle things wrong when we are trying to help them make the right decisions. We feel all the pain our children feel when they are rejected by friends or defeated in school or sports.

Before you and your parents declare war on each other, read this letter I received from a young girl who was having trouble with her mom:

Dear Barbara,

My mom is overly protective about me. She doesn't let me go hardly anywhere, see anything (like movies and TV shows). She doesn't let me listen to hardly anything, and doesn't let me wear what I want to wear. I've talked to her about it, but she feels she's not being overly protective. Do you have any suggestions for me? I'm sorry I bothered you. I hope I don't sound weird.

Sincerely, Nadine

P.S. Do you know how I can be more open with my mom? I get embarrassed when I talk to her about some things, and other things I just can't talk to her about.

Dear Nadine,

I do understand completely what you are talking about. A few years ago, I co-authored a book for parents entitled *Straight Talk for Parents: What Teenagers Wish They Could Tell You.* In this book, we took sides with teens because we felt that we understood where you were coming from. This is a new day and age from the time that your parents were teenagers. How can you possibly expect them to ever understand what it's like in this new era unless you talk to them about it?

Yes, I know what you're going to say: "I can't talk to them about it, because they expect me to live in some kind of bubble or something and not be a part of the world. I end up not talking to them about the really important things that I need to talk about because I know I'll just end up making my mom worry, and my dad will get upset and give me a lecture."

Right now, I'm not going to take sides because I want to give you some answers. Please listen with an open heart.

Sometimes it's hard to be a parent—especially a mom, because moms are usually around more of the time. Remember, your mom is the one who carried you, loved you, and prayed for you even *before* you were born. She wants only the very best for you. Moms get upset about stuff because they have this weird way of thinking that the worst that could possibly happen, will. Moms can turn every little, insignificant thing you do into a big deal!

It's things like this:

1. She looks at your messy bedroom and thinks, "Oh, my goodness, when she gets married and has her own home, her entire house will look like this room . . . and it will be all my fault because I didn't teach her properly."

2. She looks at you one day when you overslept and didn't have time to wash your hair or do anything but throw on what you had worn the day before, and she thinks, "Oh, my, the day that she goes for the most important job interview of her entire life (after her

father and I have sacrificed everything to put her through college), she will look like this. And it will all be my fault."

3. She sees you one day in the mall talking to a guy from your school. (Even *you* admit that he dresses and acts a little weird.) Your mom says, "Who was that?"

"Oh, just a friend from school," you answer.

"How long have you known him?"

"Not long."

Now you start feeling like you're in a police station under major interrogation. You think to yourself, *What's the big deal? He's just a guy in my class. It's not like I'm going to start dating him.* But you realize that your mom is now projecting what might happen in the future. She can already visualize you on your wedding day in a weird wedding gown, with your hair in dreads and a ring through your lip.

Now, you're thinking, Barbara, this can't be true. But I'm telling you, yes, it's true!

And then comes the time when she knows that you're having a problem. You are suffering with something you can't talk about. She wants to help you. She understands, even if you don't think she does, because her love for you is stronger than you could ever imagine. All she wants is for you to be happy.

I'm telling you this from personal experience. (I raised two teenagers!) It is a tremendous responsibility to be a parent. Have you ever thought of this? One day your parents went to the hospital, and a day or two later they came home with a little human being—you! This new little human was totally dependent on them for everything. Heavenly Father didn't even send a book of instructions with you. All your parents knew was that they loved you and wanted your life to be great in every way. They wanted you to have everything and every opportunity that they never had.

So they had to come up with rules, chores, restrictions, responsibilities, "time-outs," everything they could to make your life miserable, or so *you* think.

A good friend of mine, Tiffany Spencer, is a reporter for Channel 9 in Hawaii. She gave a talk about her parents, and these are some of the things she said:

Our Heavenly Father has given us the gift of choices. We are bound to make mistakes! It's not always easy to make the correct decisions, and we're going to need some help. As we strive to overcome our mistakes, an important source of strength is our parents.

My father would often tell me, "I know you don't remember, but in the pre-existence you made me promise that I'd make you do exactly what you needed to do to return to our Heavenly Father. In fact, you begged and pleaded with me, 'Please do whatever it takes!' I'm going to keep my word and make sure you return to our Heavenly Father. That's why you have to follow my rules."

Rules:

Thou shalt do thy chores every day before thou canst go out with thy friends.

Thou shalt not date until the age of sixteen, and thou wilt only be allowed to go on group dates.

Thou shalt be home by midnight, or thou wilt be grounded for a month.

Thou shalt attend thy church meetings.

Thou shalt be reverent in church, or thou shalt be forced to sit on a hard chair at home for three hours and go without dinner.

Do any of those rules sound familiar? As a teenager, I didn't understand the importance of those rules. In fact, it wasn't until I married my husband in the temple that I understood their purpose. Those guidelines helped me keep myself worthy for my mate so that I could get married in the temple for time and all eternity. Of course I made mistakes, but that's what agency is all about. Through little things great things will come to pass. You may not realize it, but the decisions you make now will affect your future.

Tiffany and her husband, Chris

Tiffany is a new mother herself now. She has all those feelings about her new little daughter that her mother had about her. Now she knows how intensely her mother loved her and wanted to keep her from harm.

Another girl, Rhonda, had been through some really rough trials due to her poor choices. But through it all, her parents loved her and were available to help her along the road of repentance when she was ready. Rhonda's father wrote her a ten-page letter, delivered to her at a summer camp. With his permission, I'd like you to share some of that letter, which shows a father's love for his daughter.

Hi, Sweetheart:

Did you have fun? Did you feel the Spirit this week? Did you make any new friends? Things have been difficult for all of us lately, but through it all there have been bright spots. A son of one of the prophets was asked what was the greatest thing his father ever taught him, and he answered, "He taught me to feel the Spirit."

I believe that if we can learn to recognize the presence of that still, small voice, as you have done, if we learn to feel it within our souls, it will be a beacon of light to guide us throughout our lives. It takes years of practice and desire and, of course, personal experience to know what the Spirit feels like.

I have always known you were very special. Your mother and I dreamed for months of starting a family. One Sunday morning, we knelt together again in prayer. The Spirit bore witness that I must start that moment to bring my life, my heart and my soul, into harmony with eternal gospel principles. Within a month, a body was begun within your mother's womb. God must have thought I was trying, because he entrusted one of his most cherished daughters into my care.

You've made life very interesting, you know. I've spent lots of nights sitting up, hoping, and praying you were okay. I have watched you experience one "first" after another, from your first step to your first heartache. I remember seeing you in tremendous pain because of the life you were living, when you fought tooth and nail against me and your mother. We wanted so much to make things better for you, but we could not.

And I think of the times since then when you have asked my advice, or when I see love light up your eyes when you talk to me. I will never be able to explain how precious those times are to me now. I remember all the blessings I have given you over the years, and how the Spirit touched me that I might know what to say. I remember so many, many things. But through it all, I knew you loved me, and I loved you—and always will.

I know God loves me, and I know he loves you. I want you to always know that I love you with all of my heart and soul. I pray for you every day. If you have patience and faith and courage, you will be blessed with the righteous desires of your heart.

I would do anything in the world for you. I plead that you can forgive me for times I have been less than gentle and for my many faults.

> *May God bless you, sweetheart.*
> *I love you, Dad*

Your parents feel a huge obligation to help you make good and wise decisions about your life. Sometimes they may get frustrated when you don't listen to or choose to accept their advice. But they do love you.

Samuel Coleridge, a poet who lived more than a century ago, was visited by an admirer one day. During the conversation, the subject got around to children.

"I believe," said the visitor, "that children should be given a free rein to think and act and thus learn at an early age to make their own decisions. This is the only way they can grow into their full potential."

"Come see my flower garden," said Coleridge, leading the man outside.

The visitor took one look and exclaimed, "Why, that's nothing but a yard full of weeds!"

"It used to be filled with roses," said Coleridge, "but this year I thought I'd let the garden grow as it willed without tending to it. This is the result."

If you were left to grow on your own, you would be "nothing but a yard full of weeds." Heavenly Father gave you parents to help you blossom and grow into the beautiful being you were meant to be.

Love your parents. Look to them for strength and support. Your parents are not perfect. They make mistakes, and they are learning along with you what it means to be a parent. But with all their faults, they do love you. See if you can talk to them and work together at making your life wonderful and productive.

Whatever happens, remember that you do have a perfect parent in our Father in Heaven. He and his Son, Jesus Christ, love you completely and perfectly. You can always talk to him, anytime, anyplace. "Search diligently, pray always, and be believing, and all things shall work together for your good" (D&C 90:24).

Your Parents Can Be Your Best Friends

Don't wait until high school is over and you're leaving home to realize that your parents truly could have been your best friends.

I asked my good friend Greta to share her feelings about her mom, who recently died of cancer. Here's what she wrote:

> My mom was my number-one fan in everything I did. She was there to support me, but sometimes I got jealous of other girls' mothers who were friends with all the girls. I would get a little angry, but we had thirteen children in my family. My mom had to go to football games or jazz band concerts. She wanted to be at everything her children did. Even if she could come only for an hour, she would still find the time to come.
>
> I remember when I was working a lot and not at home much, my mom would make sure that my work clothes were washed so that I could get some rest. She would always wake me up to make sure that I got to where I needed to go on time. When things were a bit hectic, she would sit down on the corner of my bed, and we would talk about what was going on in both our lives. I really could talk to her about important things. She would always tell me, "Greta, you can do whatever you want if you decide you want it badly enough."
>
> When my mother was struggling with cancer, I watched

her not give up. She still wanted to go to the things her kids were involved in. She was heartbroken when it got too hard for her. This was when I started to do her laundry and make sure she had enough rest. This was when I sat down on the side of her bed, and we talked about all the things going on in my busy life. She was always a great listener and had great advice.

Now that my mom is gone, I am glad that I had her as a best friend. My little sisters will never have a mom to help them through the rough teenage years. I am so grateful that I never hated my mom. We grew close with each thing that happened in both our lives.

Don't let the heat of the moment ruin your relationship with your mom. Even if your mom can't make it to all the things you do, think of how many things she does come to. She is so proud of anything you do. Take her advice as much as you can handle. Share moments with your mom even if it is just what you did that day. Don't shut your mom out of your life.

Nadine, be as brave as you can be and go to your mom. Have her read the letter you wrote to me. Then tell her you would like to talk to her. You may be surprised how much easier it is to talk to her than you think. Give it a try. You have nothing to lose, and a wonderful friend to gain.

Love, Barbara

P.S. If having a heart-to-heart talk with your mom, or telling her "I love you" or "I'm sorry," sounds like something out of your comfort zone, then try this. Become a *kigatsuku* girl.

"What?" you say.

Kigatsuku (pronounced kee-got-soo-koo).

My friend Chieko Okazaki explains that *kigatsuku* is the Japanese word for self-motivated goodness or looking for opportunities to do good. A *kigatsuku* person acts without waiting for invitations or instructions. When Chieko was a little girl and her mother was sweeping, she would run to get the dustpan and help. Or she would get a dish towel without being asked to help her mother dry the dishes. She learned to see and do what needed to be done, without being asked.

So (as in *Mission Impossible*), your assignment, should you choose to accept it, is to be a *kigatsuku* person for your parents today. Look for something that you can do to help them without being asked. By your actions, you will be telling them, "I love you."

Part 3

About Dating

Dear Barbara,
Can you please tell me what the heck goes on in a guy's brain? Why is this whole dating thing so much harder than I thought it would be?

Chapter 11

Things to Know about Guys

In an airport recently, I saw on a newsstand a paperback book that proclaimed in bold red letters: *Everything Men Know about Women,* by Dr. Allen Francis, America's foremost psychologist. In smaller letters on the cover was this comment, "Fully reveals the shocking truth"—*Daily News.*

Short reviews said: "Fiercely frank, brilliantly insightful, this work spells out everything men know about such topics as: making friends with women, romancing women, achieving emotional intimacy with women, making commitments to women. We give it five stars."—*Times Newspaper.* "Says it all."—*The Chronicle.*

I was very curious. When I opened the book, I burst out laughing. All the pages were blank.

Men and women were made to be different. It is part of God's divine plan for us—the plan of a wise and loving Creator. Instead of whining about the differences between the sexes, we need to learn to appreciate and be more tolerant of those differences. It might help us get along if we knew what those differences were.

Differences start before birth. In his seminars, Dr. Gary Smalley points out some differences between genders caused by what happens during prenatal development:

> Medical research studies have shown that in the womb, between the 18th and 26th week of gestation, something happens that forever separates the sexes. Using heat sensitive color monitors, researchers have actually observed what happens. A chemical bath of different sex-related hormones washes over a baby boy's brain, causing several important changes that never happen to the brain of a baby girl. Here is a simplified explanation of some of what happens when those chemicals hit a baby boy's system.
>
> The human brain is divided into two halves, or hemispheres, each connected by a fibrous tissue called the corpus callosum. The sex-related hormones and chemicals which flood a baby boy's brain cause the right side of the male's brain to recede slightly and destroy some of the fibers that connect the two sides. One result is that, in 85% of cases, a baby boy starts life more left-brain oriented from birth.
>
> What about little girls? From the moment of birth, because they don't go through this chemical bath, little girls are much more global or two-sided in their thinking. But it is easier for most women to tap into their right brain than a man. This is the side of the brain where the skills of having an intimate relationship reside. . . .
>
> What happens in the womb is a beautiful picture of how men and women come equipped to specialize in two different ways of thinking. This is one major reason why men and women need each other so much. (Gary Smalley, *Hidden Keys to Loving Relationships* [Paoli, Penn.: Relationships Today, Inc., 1988])

God has a perfect plan. He made us, and he created us to have differences that complement each other.

Let's look at some specific examples to explain further.

Guys	Girls
Guys are more left-brain oriented from birth. This side of the brain houses the definition of words. It favors mathematical reasoning. Guys want facts and are very solution oriented.	*Girls are bilateral, but they tend to favor the right brain. This side is the part with verbal proficiency. Girls are more involved in relating to people; they care about feelings and are sensitive and nurturing.*

When a girl just feels like being with the guy she is interested in, she might suggest, "Let's go for a walk." She shouldn't be surprised if the guy answers, "Where?" He wants the facts. She just wants to be with him.

A man came up to me after a talk once and asked, "Sister Jones, wouldn't you think that the Savior used both sides of his brain?" I answered, "Of course he did." He was the one perfect person. He was sensitive, caring, loving, giving, yet able to know the facts of all things.

Guys	Girls
Guys are into black-and-white thinking.	*Girls are very romantic. They like to analyze their relationships and get into what everything means.*

Guys buy sports magazines and how-to publications or fix-it books. They read about fishing, guns, hunting, boats, airplanes, cars, footballs, basketballs, skate- or snowboards, things that are objective, not relational.

On the other hand, teenage girls will buy magazines with topics like how to kiss, how to have a better relationship, how to get a guy to like you, how to say I love you. Women prefer magazines about people and relationships. Nearly all romance novels are purchased by women.

Guys	Girls
Guys don't cry easily or express well how they are feeling. They prefer to discover and express facts.	*Girls cry more easily and are better at describing their feelings. They can read body language and can figure out emotions.*

I asked some teenagers what they thought about a guy who gets tears in his eyes. The guys were horrified. The girls, in unison, sighed, "Ahhhhhh . . . " They like that guy even better because he is showing that he is sensitive.

Because women experience their feelings, they remember what they wore on their first date, where they went, even what music was playing. If a man remembers anything, it will probably be a solid fact. In other words, the girl asks, "Don't you remember how beautiful the restaurant was where we went for dinner on our first date?" No, he won't remember. What he will remember is . . . how much it cost!

Guys	Girls
Men can compartmentalize their brains. They seal off and separate the various parts of their lives like the watertight compartments of a submarine.	*Women's brains flow like a river. The past, present, and future all merge into one.*

If a girl and boy have an argument in the morning, for example, the boy will say, "Look, I've got to go to class right now. I'm going to be late." The argument has to end. He says they will finish talking after school. The minute he turns around and leaves, it is like that compartment in the submarine closes, Clank! He doesn't even think about it all the rest of the day.

The girl, on the other hand, can't forget. All day long she is thinking about the argument they are having. She is sure it will happen again. "I can see that if I marry this guy, this will happen again after we have our children." The past, present, and future all become one.

When they get back together, the girl says, "Now, taking up from where we left off . . . " and she's off. Because he hasn't thought about it all day, the compartment has closed. He says, "What are you talking about?"

Guys	Girls
Men are less talkative. However, they are often more boastful.	*Women are more talkative. They will sometimes talk about nothing, just to fill the silence.*

Researchers from Harvard University put little boys and girls between the ages of two and four on a playground and observed their communication skills. Amazingly, they found that 100 percent of the sounds made by girls pertained to conversation. Even though they couldn't understand all the words the little girls were saying, it was clear from their gestures and intonation that they were holding conversations.

Observing the boys, on the other hand, revealed that 68 percent of the sounds from little boys were just that—sounds. *Zooom, varooom, pshhhkkk, brrrrrrm.* Is it any wonder, then, when you see a guy and ask him about his day, he may just make a noise, "Blehhhhh!"

Studies have also shown that men speak about 12,000 words per day. Women average more than double that, at 25,000 words per day. By the time you see your date at the end of the day, he has probably used up his 12,000 words, whereas you are just getting warmed up.

Guys	Girls
Men have more energy and are able to outwork women over long periods of time. Their bodies are 40 percent muscle, with more muscles in their upper body and legs. Their ideal is 15 percent body fat. It is easier for them to lose weight.	*Women are stronger at birth. They have better immune systems. They get fewer diseases. Their bodies are 20 percent muscle. Their ideal is 24 percent body fat, with larger numbers of insulating cells that make their bodies softer.*

If a girl and a guy go on a diet together, it is disaster. He can easily drop ten pounds, while she is still struggling with losing four. He can't understand why she says losing weight is so hard. That's because he has an easier time burning all those calories since he has double the amount of muscle.

Guys	Girls
Men are very competitive. They love to watch sports. They are aggressive and goal oriented.	*Women are very personal and often not motivated by competition. They need to relate to be interested.*

Men can watch a variety of sports with great interest, even when they know little or nothing about the players. If a man wants to get a woman interested in a game, he should tell her something about the personal lives and relationships of the players.

I never liked football until I met Steve Young. Now I'm one of the biggest San Francisco 49ers fans. I had to know someone to become interested in the game. My husband, on the other hand, can enjoy watching a sport without knowing anyone on either team.

Guys	Girls
A man gains self-esteem from his job, from playing sports, from whatever he does.	*A woman has a more difficult time feeling self-worth because every aspect of her life affects her outlook. She has a relationship even with things. If the car breaks down or her curling iron blows up, she reacts with emotion. These things have betrayed her.*

Sometimes women react with more emotion than seems appropriate for the event. Girls do not view events individually. Everything is taken together. If a girl ruins a favorite dress, she might mourn for weeks. A guy, if he spills something on his favorite tie, just borrows another one from his dad.

A woman should not become upset if the man in her life seems unemotional about the things that upset her. He simply is more objective. On the other hand, he should not criticize her for "overreacting," because her emotions are truly distressing to her.

Part of God's plan is for us to go through life learning about each other's strengths and developing patience with each other's weaknesses. Together a couple can become more than each person is individually.

A final word: The Lord through his prophets has given guidelines to us in our relationships. If we go against those rules of conduct for young men and women, it often brings intense pain. The young man who wrote the following letter gave me permission to print his painful account in hopes that others could learn from it.

Dear Sister Jones,

I feel I need to presume upon your kindness and unload and ask for some advice because I have made a major mistake.

I have never seriously dated a nonmember until one girl came to church, basically at my invitation. Unfortunately we became involved. When the relationship started out, we just kissed. It never went any further until one night when I had gone over to her house with a friend. We sat around and talked until he had to leave. I felt very strongly that I needed to go with him. He felt very strongly that he should stay. Both of us ignored those feelings, and after a while, he left.

To make a long story short, that night . . . well, you know what happened. Neither of us wanted that to happen. We both talked about waiting until marriage, but the kisses made that seem so far away. That was one of the worst experiences of my life. Luckily nothing as far as pregnancy came out of it. I need advice on how to keep from slipping up again. By the way, the girl and I have never gone out again.

Thank you for letting me unload this burden momentarily on you. My greatest wish is to please use any of this to warn other teenagers you come in contact with. I don't want anybody to go through this. If my experience helps somebody out of a dead-end street, then this letter was not written in vain.

God created a strong attraction between guys and girls, but it must be saved for the right time—in marriage—where the possibility of having children is something to be happy about. You cannot play around casually with those feelings. They are too important in your life. If you want a warm, trusting relationship with someone you love, breaking the law of chastity is not the way to create it. The finest thing you can do for your future husband or wife is to become, in every way you can, the person that you want your true love to be.

But how can this be done? Aren't men and women too different? When it comes to honesty, righteousness, striving to live the gospel, and learning to be kind, those qualities cross all boundaries. They are the qualities that true sons and daughters of God can share. And best of all, they can share them together.

Chapter 12

Waiting for Sweet Sixteen

You've been told that it's a good idea to wait until you are sixteen before beginning to date. For some people, it's easy to wait, but many teens struggle with very strong feelings. Some will even go so far as to say they're in love with someone before they're even old enough, according to Church standards, to date. Then the excuses start. "They just don't understand. I'm more mature than other people my age. What we feel for each other is really love."

So why did our Church leaders pick the age of sixteen to be so magical? Are you going to suddenly grow up in just one day? Why is turning sixteen such an important time in your dating life?

I received this letter from a girl who, although she isn't officially dating, is about as close as she can get to it. And it's causing her problems at an age when she should just be enjoying life and friends. Here's what she wrote:

Dear Barbara,

My name is Jennifer, and I'm fourteen, almost fifteen. Everyone at church thinks I'm really righteous and everything, but I'm not! I've been doing some things and hanging out with some people (guys) that I shouldn't have. I've finally stopped seeing my boyfriend, and it hasn't been very easy. I think that I love my ex-boyfriend, and it's been hard living without him lately. Is it really a big deal to kiss or to meet him at the mall? I know basically what's right and what's wrong, but there is so much stuff in between.

Write back soon, Jennifer

Dear Jennifer,

I'd like to tell you about Tiffany Stoker, a young lady I worked with once who is now a good friend. Her parents were very strict about Tiffany's not dating until she was sixteen. Mr. and Mrs. Stoker started teaching this principle early. They learned that even certain kinds of kissing could lead to immorality. They were determined to guide their children past that heartache.

When Tiffany was only eleven years old, her parents came to her one day with a dare. They said, "Tiffany, we'll give you three hundred dollars if you don't kiss a boy or allow yourself to be kissed until you are sixteen."

Three hundred dollars! Wow! At the age of eleven, three hundred dollars sounded like a ton of money. Besides, Tiffany was shy. Ugh! Boys were kind of yucky anyway. She didn't foresee any problem with committing not to be kissed. But her parents were serious. "Tiffany, we really mean it." Tiffany gladly promised. This was going to be an easy three hundred bucks.

Four years passed. No problems. Tiffany was just as determined as she had been at age eleven. The money was as good as in her pocket.

Then, at age fifteen, Tiffany began to notice a boy, Josh, who she thought was really, really cute. She could tell that he liked her, too. Now what? They didn't date, of course. Tiffany wasn't sixteen yet. So Tiffany and Josh spent time together studying with their friends at the library or watching videos at her house with her family. Every time she saw him, the idea of a quick goodnight kiss seemed pretty nice. Maybe it was worth giving up the three hundred dollars.

Tiffany went to her mother. "Mom," she said,"I have to tell you honestly that three hundred dollars doesn't seem like that much money anymore. I don't think it's worth it."

Her mom had the perfect answer: "Okay, how about five hundred dollars? Are you strong enough to finish what you started, or will you quit?"

Now, five hundred dollars is really a lot of money. But money wasn't meaning as much to Tiffany as Josh did. Her mother knew her daughter inside and out. She knew Tiffany might not stick to their agreement for money but would do anything to avoid being a quitter.

Somehow Tiffany's deal with her parents spread around her high school. Other students started to tease her. Tiffany and Josh were the perfect couple, but now everyone seemed to think they were weird.

Pretty soon, the way stories go, the details started to change. "Is it true, Tiffany, that you'll get a thousand dollars if you don't kiss until you are sixteen?" "Tiffany, I heard you'll get a brand-new Mercedes." Tiffany's only defense was humor. "No," she replied. "Actually I'll get five thousand dollars or a cruise. Isn't that great?"

Fortunately, Josh was not just cute, he was considerate. Once he gave her a little kiss on the cheek. Tiffany ran all the way home to confer with her parents. "Did that count? Is the bet still on?"

That wasn't the kind of kiss her parents were thinking about. The bet was still on.

That year, the Junior Prom was held on Tiffany's sixteenth birthday. Tiffany felt like she and Josh would be on display the whole night. She was nervous. Why had she ever imagined that she wanted to kiss anybody, including Josh?

Josh picked her up for the dance and gave her a long package with red lip stickers plastered all over it. Attached to the outside of the package, under the bow, was a drinking straw, with a balloon on one end. She blew on the straw, and the balloon inflated into gigantic lips. She didn't know whether to laugh or cry.

Tiffany opened the package. It was filled with chocolate kisses. Now she could laugh. That was one of the things she liked best about Josh—he was so easy to laugh with.

That night Tiffany collected five hundred dollars and her first kiss.

Tiffany and Josh continued to be a couple. But they didn't hang all over each other. They both had interests that occupied a lot of their time. They saw each other every once in a while during the summers. Josh was a year older than Tiffany. He was attending college on a football scholarship as she finished high school. Tiffany was studying dancing and singing. They had their own goals, and each respected the other person as they both spent time working toward those goals.

When Josh entered college, there was a lot of drinking on his campus. But Tiffany didn't worry. Josh had always demonstrated self-control, so she had no doubts that he could handle the peer pressure and remain strong.

Tiffany was also a strong person. She hadn't given in on the kiss, and she certainly was not going to give in to other pressures around her now. On Tiffany's eighteenth birthday, Josh gave her a framed picture of two small children kissing. He signed it, "Thanks for the first kiss. Love, Josh."

When Josh left on his mission, he said, "Tiffany, I don't want you to wait for me." Tiffany said, "Thanks, I wasn't planning to."

Josh gave himself 100 percent to his mission. He wrote Tiffany occasionally, and she answered in the same way. "I dated a lot," says Tiffany. "I saw other guys, and it was good because I found out what I really liked about Josh.

In 1995, Tiffany was crowned Miss California. She was described in a newspaper article as "gutsy" for choosing as her platform issue "sexual abstinence for teenagers." Later, after her talent performance at the Miss America pageant, a New York agent called her to audition for the part of Kim in the Broadway musical *Showboat*. She returned from the audition in New York with an offer to play that part in the Vancouver, Canada, company that would move to Los Angeles a few months later.

What do you dream for your own life? You may not be a Miss

America or play a part in a big musical production. But Tiffany's happiest day did not take place on a stage, in front of thousands of fans. In fact, there were just a few people she loved with her that day, in the temple, where she and Josh were married.

A day like this starts with a choice, a little decision like not dating until the age of sixteen or saving that first kiss for the right time. A choice like that gives you time to grow up a little. You will have time to have fun just being friends.

Will some guys think you've made a stupid decision? Maybe. But if they do, and if they give you a hard time about it, then they might not be the kind of guys you should pay attention to anyway. Guys who are worth caring about will recognize that you're someone special. They will know that you value yourself, and everyone wants the person he or she likes to be valuable.

I hope that this story will inspire you to follow your standards during the time you are dating. I promise that you'll be glad you did.

Love, Barbara

P.S. I want to end this letter with Tiffany's own words. She said the following things when she was seventeen years old, in a talk she was asked to give by the student body at a high school in her area.

I made a decision early on that I would not sacrifice my values for the sake of popularity. When I was nominated Homecoming Queen and then Most Popular Girl of my graduating class, I knew my decision had not prevented me from a wonderful high school experience full of friends and fun.

When older generations hand us condoms in school with the reasoning, "We know you are going to have sex, so here, use these," they aren't doing us any favors. Consider the high failure rate of condoms (they fail one in six times).

Would you let your child go skydiving with five friends if you knew that at least one parachute would not open? We are not bashful about saying, "Don't drink," or "Don't do drugs." Sex is not illegal like drugs, but premarital sex is just as damaging.

We must realize that the crushes we experience as teenagers are just dress rehearsals for the mature love that comes later in life. We need to distinguish between real love, where we want the best for the other person, and lust, where we just *want* the other person.

We, the young people of the '90s, have the power to say "No!" to things that destroy. I believe in abstinence. My boyfriend, who plays football for Stanford University, has made the same decision, and because of this we have respect for each other that many relationships lack. It's not easy, but we help each other.

Be like Tiffany. It's a good choice.

Chapter 13

Dating Is Supposed to Be Fun

The next time you feel like you'll never have a date with a guy you really like, just remember that the whole idea of dating is not the same the world over. In many societies, even today, marriages are prearranged.

Just imagine this: One night your parents invite the neighbors over for dinner. The two couples are best friends, and the neighbors have a son about your age. That night, as they are visiting and talking about how much fun you two toddlers are having together, they decide that when you are both eighteen you will be married.

A formal marriage contract is drawn up and signed by both sets of parents. They don't ask you, because as a three-year-old you don't have many opinions on marriage. You're more interested in whacking your fiancé on the head with your doll.

However, by the first grade, you are beginning to wonder if this was such a good idea. Every day after lunch your fiancé wets his pants. It's so embarrassing.

By junior high school, he is a foot shorter than you and never seems to wash his hair. Worst of all, he snorts when he laughs, and he says things to his friends that you can't quite hear. They all look over at you and start punching your fiancé on the arm. You don't even want to know what they said.

By high school, he dresses like a total nerd and embarrasses you in the cafeteria by eating everything with his hands. He never wants to talk about anything but computer games. Worst of all, since you are engaged, you can't date anyone else.

Aren't you glad this won't happen to you? It makes the weird things that happen in the dating years seem not so bad after all.

Dating is one of those things that some people seem to have a talent for, whereas others seem to mess up every romance before it even starts. In this chapter, we're going to talk about some dating secrets, some things you should know about boys.

Here is a letter I received from a young girl:

Dear Sister Jones,

I'm writing you to ask some advice. Right now I have a boyfriend. We have been going out for about a month. My mom and my grandma tell me to "keep 'em guessing." Well, how do I do that? I don't have the slightest idea! I always tell my boyfriend how I feel about him. Is that wrong? Sometimes I read him parts of my diary. He tells me how he feels about me. It's all really good, I mean, he's already told me he loves me, and he was very serious when he said it.

But, Sister Jones, it seems like there is no "spark" between us anymore. Do you know what I mean? So how can I get this relationship going again? I want to learn about boys and how to "keep 'em guessing." Do you have any ideas?

Love, Laura

At first, it sounds like Laura's habit of telling her boyfriend absolutely everything would be the honest way to relate to him. I've heard girls say that they don't want to "play games," that they want a guy to know how they feel all the time. But that style of relating also becomes overly possessive and too intimate for just a dating relationship. Dating is a time to get to know each other in a relaxed, easygoing atmosphere. Many of those truly personal things Laura was saying to her boyfriend should have been reserved for the man she will eventually marry.

What a Boy Wants in a Girlfriend

Since I was never a teenage boy, I can't tell you exactly what they are thinking. But I do speak to classes that have a lot of guys in them, so I decided to ask them to tell me exactly what they are looking for. I asked them to write down at least ten things they are looking for in an eternal companion. Yes, I said *eternal companion*. After all, isn't that what dating is ultimately all about: finding that one person we will be with for eternity?

Sometimes just thinking about eternity makes your head hurt. You can hardly decide what to wear tomorrow, let alone make a decision of eternal significance. But dating is going to help you make that decision.

Somewhere in this world there's a special guy who is going to be married to you one day. At this moment, he has a list something like this:

I want . . .

a girl who is really smart and applies herself.

a girl who respects me.

a girl who has a firm testimony of the gospel.

a girl who is really good with kids.

a girl who is patient.

a girl who has a good sense of humor.

a girl who has earned her Young Womanhood Recognition award.

a girl who is physically fit.

a girl who is fun to be with.

a girl who is spontaneous.

a girl who is rich. (No, not really rich. He wants a girl who, if needed when times get tough, could go out and help him support the family because she's gone to college and earned a degree or learned a trade.)

a girl who loves me.

a girl who looks nice.

a girl who is optimistic and has a good attitude.

a girl who likes to do the things I like to do.

The list goes on, but this should be enough to show you that the things on his list are almost exactly the same as the things on your list. And if you want to find this guy, you need to be doing the same things you want him to be doing. In other words, you need to become exactly the type of person you are looking for.

If You Want to Ruin a Romance

1. Be a doormat. Doormats are made to be walked on, and sooner or later that's what happens. My daughter, Wendy, really liked Bill, the captain of the football team. She did everything for him—baked brownies and decorated his locker with balloons for his birthday. She said, "Mom, I like spoiling him."

"Yes," I asked, "but does he do anything for you? Back off a minute." If Bill, or whoever, doesn't care enough about you to do some of the little endearing things you like, don't go overboard in the opposite direction. Don't make your friendship a one-way street. It doesn't work.

2. Take him for granted. The truth is that it's harder for guys to do things for girls. If he does one little thing, make a big deal of it and let him know how wonderful his gesture made you feel. You may need to drop a few hints so that he'll know some nice things he can do for you!

3. Get hung up on three little words. It's much easier for a girl to be demonstrative, to say, "I love you," than it is for a male of any age. The words tend to stick in their throats. Give him time. If it's right, one day he'll say those words.

4. Be Velcro. Don't be totally dependent, the clinging vine. At an Especially for Youth conference, I once heard a guy say of a girl coming toward him and his friends, "Oh, no! Miss Velcro!" Do not—I repeat, *do not*—be Miss Velcro. Scenario: You start dating a cute guy. You like him. He comes out of his classroom, and there you are! He goes to his locker, and there you are! He goes to lunch, and there you are! After school he goes to the parking lot, and guess what? The minute he gets home, you're calling him on the telephone. Not smart. Let him have to put forth some effort.

5. *Chase a guy.* If you don't take away anything else from this chapter on dating, remember this hint: Don't ever chase somebody you happen to like. Be subtle. There is a line in an old song that goes, "A boy chases a girl until she catches him." The thrill of the chase is built into the man. Once you are caught, the game is over. The guy will move on.

Don't be conquered. He won't start taking you for granted if he sees that you still have interests and activities that don't include him.

You may not like this. "I don't want to pretend," you may say. "I just can't stand to play games." But think of it this way: A running horse is always more beautiful than one in a stall. If you are always working on your own goals and your own interests, you will be a more interesting person, someone a guy will want to know better.

Keep these hints in mind, and remember: dating is supposed to be *fun!*

Chapter 14

Make a Marriage for Eternity

 Have you noticed how many Latter-day Saint kids wear CTR rings? Maybe you have one too. What does the CTR stand for? Choose the right, of course.

But do you believe it? Do you believe that if you choose the right, it will always pay off? In fact, our Heavenly Father has made us a promise. He said, "I, the Lord, am bound when ye do what I say; but when ye do not what I say, ye have no promise" (D&C 82:10).

The Lord has made you a promise! Think of it. It's so amazing. The Lord of heaven and earth has made you a promise. And if you want that promise to come true, you have to keep your part. You have to continue to choose the right, trusting in him and his timetable. This applies even to such things as dating and finding the person you should marry.

Dear Barbara,

I've never had a boyfriend, and everyone I know has had one before. I don't have any self-confidence.

The day I received my patriarchal blessing was the most beautiful day of my life because I was promised and blessed with so many wonderful things. The blessing I especially enjoy is the one that says, "I bless you that in the due time of the Lord you will be able to have a companion, someone prepared for you, who will be worthy of your wonderful and sweet spirit, and someone who can love you and be with you throughout all your life, and that you will have a marriage for time and eternity in the temple."

I get goose bumps and cry every time I read that because it's so wonderful. I feel, though, that I don't deserve it, like I'm not pretty enough to ever get a husband. I'm not good enough. It would be a miracle if someone would love me enough to marry me. Yet, somehow, I know it will happen, and I think to myself, There's a guy out there somewhere that the Lord is preparing just for me! That really makes me feel so loved and special. Then there are those times when I doubt it and think it will never really happen.

Can you help me, Sister Jones? Thank you for listening.

Love always, Janice

Dear Janice,

I couldn't wait to answer your letter because I just returned from visiting some friends in another state, and while I was there, this couple, Tiffany and Chris, were asked to give a talk in sacrament meeting. They told about how they grew up knowing each other, but it was from following their parents' rules that they came to be married in the temple.

I asked Chris to write his talk down, and now I share his story—their story—with you.

I was taught by my parents from a very young age to plan on being married in the temple. I remember my parents asking often in our family prayers that the Lord would bless their sons and future daughters-in-law that they would be prepared by the Lord's hand to enter his holy house to be sealed for all eternity.

I met my eternal companion when I was a senior in high

school. Her name was Tiffany Banks. I was attending my last youth conference before I went on my mission, and it took me all night to get up enough nerve to ask her to dance. We went out a few times that summer. I felt deep down inside that she was to be my eternal mate. My prayers changed from "Please prepare my wife . . ." to "Please prepare Tiffany."

We didn't date seriously until I had been home from my mission for a year. We talked about marriage, and we both felt really good about each other. Then she told me she was going to Israel with the BYU Study Abroad program. She was gone for six long months. I didn't date anyone else while she was gone. I would even go to the temple with her father.

I remember one evening in particular. I was sitting in the celestial room of the temple thinking about Tiffany. I felt compelled to offer a prayer to our Heavenly Father asking him to confirm my feelings that Tiffany would be my eternal companion. I felt a warm assurance that I had made the right decision.

But just before Tiffany was to return from Israel, her letters began tapering off. I told myself she was just busy. When she got home, she had changed, but only for the better. However, she had new friends. Soon I was competing for her time. She would go out with her friends and didn't give me the time of day. We finally agreed to not see each other or talk for a couple of weeks so we could both have time to think.

I was so confused and depressed. I went to the Lord again; I got down on my knees and asked if she was the person I should marry. At the conclusion of my prayer, I got up, opened my scriptures, and immediately found my answer: "Verily, verily, I say unto you, if you desire a further witness, cast your mind upon the night that you cried unto me in your heart, that you might know concerning the truth of these things. Did I not speak peace to your mind concerning the matter? What greater witness can you have than from God?" (D&C 6:22-23).

The minute I read this, I found myself reflecting back to that night in the temple when I had asked a similar question. I had received my answer then, but when I encountered difficulty, my lack of faith caused me to doubt our Heavenly Father's wisdom. I was patient, and things between us worked out.

My wife and I were sealed in the Salt Lake Temple, and we have a beautiful marriage and a baby daughter. Every day I thank my Father in Heaven for a wonderful relationship that will continue through the eternities. I'm thankful for good parents who taught me well and for personal revelation that provides us with opportunities to be taught firsthand by the Spirit.

When we follow the Lord in everything we do, then things will work for our good. Most of the time we cannot see why we have to go through a particular hard thing. "Why don't I have a date for the prom?" "Why doesn't the person I really like seem to like me back?" The answers are not simple. Only the Lord sees the whole plan. We must have faith that he will guide us, and we must stay worthy to have his guiding influence in our lives.

I want to tell you one more story about a romance that led to the temple. I know a lot of great details about this story because it happened to my daughter, Wendy.

Let me first give you a picture of what Wendy is like. When she was in the first grade, her father asked her what she wanted to be when she grew up. Wendy attended a Catholic school in San Francisco. She loved her teacher, who happened to be pregnant. She also adored the principal of the school, Sister Mary Carmella. And Wendy adored the eighth-grade cheerleaders. So when her father asked, Wendy answered, "I'm going to be a pregnant, nun, cheerleader!"

Wendy has never outgrown her enthusiasm for life. However, she had a hard time in high school. She was the only LDS girl in her school. She wanted very much to fit in, to be accepted, to be popular. She had a hard time with friends who were beginning to experiment with drinking. She faced some hard times when a close friend tried to drag her down into a lifestyle she could not accept. Wendy was miserable and gained a lot of weight, which made her feel even worse about herself. A close friend was killed during their junior year. Wendy was dating the captain of the football team, and he dumped her right before the prom. A huge problem occurred when her special friendship with a camp counselor she had known for six years ended abruptly. She told me later that at one point during those years she had even considered killing herself. Everything she tried to do to fit in at school just pulled her further off track. As a mother, all I could do was pray.

After her junior year, we insisted that Wendy go to New Guinea with Team Missions International. She had to work very hard and live in primitive conditions, but her love of life returned. She came back healthy in body and attitude. She really knew she was a daughter of a Heavenly Father who loved her. She had seen him answer her prayers. As she entered her senior year, she said it was going to be the best year of her life. And she made it happen.

Wendy was happy, and she was grateful. She had lost the weight in New Guinea because she was working and exercising every day. She really felt good about herself. She was a varsity cheerleader. She earned her track letter. She was a student-body officer. She was in charge of the prom. She had a good friend all through that year, a friend who was becoming a serious boyfriend.

I soon realized that this friend, Jeff, was an atheist. He also drank a lot. As the year came to a close, Wendy confided in me that this was the person she was going to marry as soon as he finished college. They were very much in love. Again I prayed, as only a mom can pray, that she would find an eternal companion who would help her fulfill the life Heavenly Father had planned for her.

That summer, Wendy went to BYU to be a counselor for the Especially for Youth program. She and her boyfriend had promised to write each other all of that time. After several weeks, I heard through the grapevine that he wasn't getting any letters from her.

One evening, the phone rang. It was Wendy. She said: "Mom, I found him. My eternal companion. He's gorgeous, tall, blond hair, and he's such a spiritual guy. He's a . . . *returned missionary!*"

I was thinking, *Wow, this truly is an answer to prayer.* I was looking toward heaven, mouthing the words, "Thank you." I asked how long she had been dating him. She said, "Well, we've only had one date. But Mom, I just know he is my eternal companion."

It's a good thing she couldn't see through the telephone wires. I could feel myself rolling my eyes. I told her to keep me posted.

A couple of weeks passed. One night she called crying. I asked her what was wrong. She said, "Mom, I thought he would be my eternal companion. Well, he's dating this other girl. Mom, there's nothing special about her, except . . . she's a returned missionary!" Wendy began crying even harder, "Oh, Mom, where did I go wrong?"

I thought, *After all these years, here's my chance to really give some advice.* I asked Wendy if she remembered back when she was a Beehive how her teacher had made her write down a list of five things she was looking for in an eternal companion. I asked her what they were. She said, "Well, (sniff, sniff) number one, he had to be a returned missionary. Number two, he had to be a good provider for his family. Number three, he had to be really, really spiritual. Number four, he had to love his mother. And number five, he had to love children and be a good father."

I said, "Wendy, unless you can be like that person and fill all those qualities *you* are looking for, you will never find that special guy."

At the end of the summer, Wendy told her father and me that she was going to cosmetology school. The reason: "If ever my husband needs me to help while he finishes college or gets his master's degree, I will have this trade so that I can help put him through school." She was also following her talents and interests. She made the highest grades in her class. She won awards in Los Angeles for makeup and hairstyles in big shows. She excelled in the profession of her choice.

Right before she graduated, she called us and said, "Mom, Dad, I've made another decision. I just put in my mission papers. I prayed and asked Heavenly Father to give me the very hardest mission that he wanted to give me."

I thought, *Oh, Wendy, you had better watch out what you pray for.* Sure enough, she was called to Honduras, a country where she would often be without even running water, let alone the luxuries we have here.

Wendy had a hard time in the MTC learning a new language. At first, it was difficult in the mission field. She had cultural differences to get used to, and not being able to speak the language fluently made it more frustrating. In her letters, I saw her beginning to grow and blossom into a very spiritual, loving person, a young woman with depth.

Wendy was becoming everything on her list. She could help provide for her family. She was gaining great spirituality. She loved her mother, and she wrote about the children she had come to love and care for.

The summer when Wendy left on her mission, I co-directed a camp called *Be the Best You* on the BYU campus. It was the first year of the camp. We had about thirty-five college-age counselors. At the counselor training meeting, I saw one young man across the room. He was *so cute!* I asked my co-director, Clark Smith, about him. Clark said his name was Shane Adamson.

I walked up to him and introduced myself. I said, "Hi, I'm Sister Barbara Barrington Jones, and I just wanted you to know that you are one of the cutest guys I have ever seen in my life." He blushed.

I watched this young man all throughout the camp and saw what an outstanding person he was. He had served his mission in Japan. He was so good with his group of ten boys. I watched him interact with special-needs kids and elderly people. I thought to myself, *This is just a good guy.*

The following January, Shane wrote me a letter.

Dear Sister Jones,

I had a wonderful time being a counselor for your camp. I was wondering if you might write me a letter of recommendation so that I could be a counselor next summer also.

I wrote back right away.

Dear Shane,

Not only will I write you a letter of recommendation to be a counselor for our camp, but . . . How would you like to marry my daughter?

Shane wrote back:

Dear Sister Jones,

Thank you so much for the letter of recommendation. And regarding your daughter, I didn't know that you had a daughter. But [now he really got extra points from this next sentence], if your daughter is anything like you, I would date her in a heartbeat.

I sent him Wendy's address, and he wrote her a postcard. They wrote back and forth for eight months. They had never seen each other. I was afraid to tell Wendy how cute he was. (Sometimes she doesn't think that my idea of cute is the same as hers.) I thought it would be better not to say anything.

Shane and Wendy really got to know each other through their letters and built a relationship based on friendship. They found out a lot about each other: their likes, their dislikes, how they felt about things. Just before Wendy was to come home, they decided to exchange pictures.

Then things went into an uproar. There were terrorist threats, and Wendy had to come home two weeks before her release date. Shane's picture arrived, but with the mission in chaos, her zone leaders saw their chance to play a little trick. They took Shane's picture out of the envelope and replaced it with a photo of funny-looking parents, tons of kids, and the family pet, a pit bull.

Wendy opened the letter on the plane on the way home. When she got off the plane, she said, "Mom, I can't believe that this is Shane. He painted an entirely different picture of himself and his family."

I took one look at the picture and knew exactly what had happened. Inside I was laughing so hard, but I didn't say a word.

We called a counselor meeting for a couple of weeks after Wendy's return home. I told Shane and Wendy that I would introduce them at the meeting. My co-director and I decided to play a fabulous practical joke. We told all the other counselors that the meeting was at 3:00; then I told Shane it was at 3:30. We fixed up our meeting room to look like a wedding chapel. We lined the chairs up in rows on both sides. We borrowed a wedding gown, a veil, a bouquet of silk flowers, and a cassette tape of the wedding march.

When Shane knocked on the door, I opened it and grabbed him so he wouldn't run away. Someone turned the music on. It was the wedding march! Clark Smith, posing as a minister, was standing in front dressed in a tuxedo shirt, a coat, a cummerbund, a bow tie, bermuda shorts, and thongs.

We walked down the aisle with all the counselors laughing. Shane was turning fifty shades of red. Clark said, "Dearly beloved, we are gathered here today to join this man and this woman . . . Someone bring in the bride." You could see Shane's eyes getting bigger and bigger.

Out of the bathroom walked Wendy in the borrowed wedding gown. With the wedding march playing, she walked down the aisle. Shane and Wendy couldn't even look at each other, they were so embarrassed. Wendy whispered, "They made me do it." When they were standing side by side, Shane glanced at her, shook her hand, and said, "Nice to meet you."

Clark started the ceremony. "Wendy Jones, will you take this man to be your lawful and happy friend through cheap dates and dollar movies for the next couple of months?" They both said their I dos, and Clark pronounced them "Friends with potential."

Shane and Wendy forgave us, and they went on their first date. They dated from October until the following February. On Valentine's Day, in the snow on Temple Square, Shane knelt and asked Wendy to marry him. Of course, she said yes.

On the third of July, Shane and Wendy were married for time and all eternity. Heavenly Father had prepared them for each other, and they had prepared themselves by doing the things they had been taught.

Janice, I'm sorry this letter has been so long, but I just wanted you to know that even though you cannot see into the future, you can begin right now to prepare yourself for the person you will marry. Instead of worrying about where he is and what he is doing, spend your time working at becoming the type of person you are looking for. I know that it will make you happy and give you confidence. Then, just when you are ready, you will have wonderful experiences that will prepare you for your future.

Thanks for writing. Let me know what you are doing and how you feel about the things you learn.

Love, Barbara

P.S. I know that you will love these scrapbook pages that Wendy and I put together. If you prepare yourself well and trust in the Lord, someday you will be able to make pages for your scrapbook like these.

Shane became a hunter

And Wendy wore "Buffy Tails"

Shane calls this his "nerd" picture

*And Wendy has one too
. . . but they had never met*

Shane went to high school

And Wendy did too

*Shane entered the Missionary
Training Center*

*And Wendy did too
. . . but still they had never met*

Shane in Japan on his mission

Wendy in Honduras on her mission

*In the Practical Joke of the Century, they
finally met!*

Their first date

Shane proposed on Valentine's Day

And they were married for time and all eternity

Part 4

Looking Good, Feeling Great

Dear Barbara,
Some girls look so put together all the time. I don't have a lot of money to spend, but I wonder, could you tell me some ways I could look and feel better?

I Just Feel So Ugly

"I just feel so ugly." Have you ever said this about yourself? Have you ever thought it?

It is a shocking thing to say because it is so hurtful when you say it or believe it about yourself. You've heard people say that it's what's inside that counts. But you may think that the pretty girls still seem to get all the attention and good things in life. They have all the friends and all the dates. So what really counts?

To help us understand better, let's talk about something really important—the temple. Imagine what you would feel if you and your family drove up to the temple, and there was nothing but an asphalt parking lot around it. Picture it: over in the corner of the parking lot, there's a pile of empty cans and old newspapers that have blown around; no one has bothered to pick them up. Someone has abandoned a car, and it is sitting with flat tires, just rusting in the weather. Where there were once beautiful fountains, all that is left are dry, decaying ponds. The outside of the temple was once white, but now it's all grimy and dirty. Someone has even spray-painted some graffiti on the walls. There are no well-kept lawns, no trees, no flowers. The parking lot even smells of rotting garbage. The exterior of the building has chipped in places, and the whole thing looks run-down.

Once you are inside, however, the temple is just as beautiful as ever. It almost seems like a palace, with beautiful crystal chandeliers, gilt-edged mirrors, and elegant carpeting and upholstered furniture. Everything is spotlessly clean and well cared for.

When you ask what has happened, someone tries to explain that the exterior doesn't matter. After all, the important thing is what happens inside the temple. But that just doesn't seem right. It makes you sick that the outside of the temple looks so bad when what happens inside is so wonderful. It doesn't seem respectful.

Thankfully, that is not the way things really are. The outsides of our temples, including the grounds, are as beautiful as we can make them. Every temple is meticulously cared for, inside and out, because we want the beauty of the exterior to reflect just a portion of what we feel about the inside.

The most important thing about being in the temple is the special feeling of peace, of closeness to our Heavenly Father, that comes when we are there. It is the place to learn more about Christ, to make sacred covenants, and to be sealed to our families for time and all eternity. The most important things in the whole world happen inside the walls of the temple.

If the exteriors of our temples and temple grounds were neglected, would people who drove by ever want to know what special things happened on the inside? We carefully care for the outside of our temples and make them gleaming and beautiful because we have respect for what goes on inside. We value the temple, so we care for its outward appearance.

Shouldn't it be the same for our bodies? Our bodies are gifts from God, with great potential for righteousness. We understand that the most important things about us happen on the inside, but because we have great respect for the things God has given us, we should care for and make this temple beautiful also.

Sometimes the concept of taking care of our external appearance may appear to some to be in direct conflict with the teachings of the gospel. We have been taught in the scriptures, "For the Lord seeth not as man seeth; for man looketh on the outward appearance, but the Lord looketh on the heart" (1 Samuel 16:7). However, our prophets have often encouraged us to pay attention to our appearance and try to improve it.

President David O. McKay said in his book *Gospel Ideals* (Salt Lake City: Deseret Book, 1976): "It is not my purpose to discourage efforts to enhance physical beauty. When given by birth, it should be nurtured in childhood, cherished in girlhood, and protected in womanhood. When not inherited, it should be developed and sought after in every legitimate and healthful manner" (p. 450).

President Spencer W. Kimball went into a little more detail. "You need to evaluate yourselves carefully, take a careful inventory of your habits, your speech, your appearance, your weight, and your eccentricities, if you have any. Take each item and analyze it. Can you make some sacrifices to be acceptable? You must be the judge.

"Is your dress too old-fashioned, or too revealing, or too extreme? . . . Have you made yourself attractive physically—well groomed, well dressed—and attractive mentally—engaging, interesting? . . .

"Continue to make yourself attractive physically, mentally, spiritually, and emotionally" ("There is a Purpose in Life," *New Era*, September 1974, 7).

It is clearly appropriate to do the things we can to make our bodies attractive as well as to work on what we are inside. The truth is that nearly everyone can make a good impression by being well-groomed and neatly dressed. We cannot all look like models, even though a high percentage of teenage girls wish they did. We can learn to do what we can and then stop worrying so much about the things we can't change.

This letter I received is so typical of the attitude I have discovered in some young women.

Dear Barbara,

I come from a small town and a very religious family. I had some tragedies happen in my life, and they caused me to become really confused inside. I even went to counseling. My parents told me to say my prayers, but somehow I didn't think Heavenly Father was listening to me. My self-esteem was so low! It was almost impossible to ever think of being confident.

Every day I would look in the mirror and say, "I'm so ugly!" Finally, I thought, "What's the use?" That's when things got worse. My room got messier than ever, and I didn't care one bit what I looked like, either. I would wear clothes that had been on the bottom of the closet for days. I would hardly ever shower or even brush my teeth. My hair would get so oily that my face began to break out. When I was in junior high, I had loved sports, but now I just sat in my room. The more depressed I got, the darker I would make my room. I didn't feel like eating regular meals, so I lived on candy bars and Cokes. I felt like my life had been put into a blender.

To top everything off, we found out that my dad had leukemia (a form of cancer). He had months of radiation and chemotherapy. Then, one day while I was home, I heard my dad fall in the bathroom. I ran in and found him lying on the floor. His nose was bleeding, and his eyes were glassy. I knew that I needed to get him off the floor, but he is a very big man. I tried to lift him, but I couldn't. I started crying. My dad was trying to tell me something, but I could hardly hear him. I put my ear close to his mouth. He whispered, "Sweetie, if I don't make it, please remember how much I love you, but you need to change the way you are living."

Then he lost consciousness. I've never prayed harder in my life. I told Heavenly Father that I would change if he would just give me the power to help my dad. To this day, I don't know how I did it, but I lifted my dad off the floor. I called 911, and they Life-Flighted him to the hospital. He made it through one more time.

I had made a pact with God, and he had helped me. Now I needed to keep my part of the bargain. I started with my room. It was a DISASTER! After it was clean, my mom took me to the paint store, bought some paint, and helped me paint it from top to bottom. She made new curtains, and we found a pretty bedspread. What a difference!

I started doing better in school. Next, I joined the track team, and my coach helped me with a healthy eating plan. I started reading in my scriptures and praying every day. But I still looked in the mirror and said, "I'm so ugly! What difference does it make? I'll never be beautiful."

Finally, with the courage that I got from reading certain parts of your book, I decided to talk to my mom about how ugly I felt. And this is why I'm writing you this letter, because what she said changed everything for me, and if it helped me, it might help other girls who feel like I did.

My mom reminded me that our bodies are like the temple. I finally had a new vision of what I needed to do, and I did it. I fixed up the grounds of my temple. I know now that your outside appearance has a lot to do with how you feel about yourself. I just want you to know that I'm grateful that you took the time to care about girls like me. I can't wait to graduate from cosmetology school so that I can help other girls to feel better about themselves.

With love and gratitude, Jacci

Dear Jacci,

What a fabulous letter! I am so happy for you. It sounds like you have made so many positive changes in your life. With your permission, I'd like to print your letter. Every day I get letters from teenage girls wanting to know all kinds of things, from how to have a better complexion, to what colors to wear, to how to care for and wear their hair. Some say they feel so ugly that they have nearly given up, as you once did.

I just want you to remember one really important thing about your appearance. The Lord sees you as a precious and beautiful child of his. He knows your heart. We all know that what's inside is the most important, but, as you are now discovering, it's difficult to get people to want to know what's inside if we don't make an effort on our outward appearance.

The problem with many girls is that they think they are not pretty. The truth is that sometimes we can't see ourselves for who we really are. One girl wrote to me, "My mom says that I'm pretty, but how can you trust your mom?"

A girl I met in Newcastle, Australia, wrote me a letter saying, "I'm not really pretty." And this is the photo she enclosed. She is so pretty, but *she* can't see it. Sometimes we can't even see ourselves accurately

at all. We get caught up in looking for flaws, and soon the flaws are all we see.

I read in a magazine about a woman who had felt unattractive as a teenager. She said: "I learned to make the best of my good features. God blessed me with great hair and pretty eyes, so I play up these features and do the best I can with the rest. I'll never appear on any magazine covers, but I feel good about myself."

You mentioned that you hoped your self-worth would increase if you looked better. I need to give you a little warning. Looking your best will give you some confidence, which might help you relax and be yourself. But feelings of self-worth come from inside. If you take care of your appearance at the beginning of each day, and then forget about how you look and pay attention to others, you will find your best self.

Giving service to others and taking care of your own appearance are not opposites. You can do both. If you do all things in righteousness, then blessings, especially the blessing of feeling good about yourself, will come.

In the following chapters, I'll be sharing with you some advice from some experts on improving your appearance. You mentioned that money is a problem. You'll find that the advice I'll be giving you mostly involves simple things you can do without spending more than you usually do. I hope you will gain a lot of knowledge from the answers in the following chapters. I'll be thinking of you.

Love, Barbara

P.S. Write out a list of all your good qualities, including your good physical qualities. If you can't write out this list yourself, ask a close friend or your parents to help you. Then keep a copy with you all the time. Whenever you start to feel down on yourself, get the list out and read it.

You can still work to improve things about yourself, but don't focus on your imperfections and forget about all of your good qualities. If you are going to spend all that time worrying about your bad points, be sure to give equal time to thinking about your good points. This isn't pride. It's a way to think more realistically about yourself.

Add Color
to Your Life

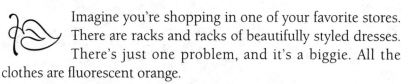 Imagine you're shopping in one of your favorite stores. There are racks and racks of beautifully styled dresses. There's just one problem, and it's a biggie. All the clothes are fluorescent orange.

You hurry to another store. It's the same, all orange.

You wake up. Thank goodness, it was just a nightmare. You don't have to be limited in something so amazing and interesting as color. The world is full of great colors, and by knowing and choosing those that look best on you, you can design your wardrobe to bring out the best in your looks. Best of all, it doesn't cost a cent more to choose colors that express something about your personality. And you certainly don't have to throw out everything you own and start over.

Learning about color is a simple yet effective place to start when you want to understand how to look your best. And the impact is immediate. Wear the right color for your complexion and hair color, and the moment you put it on, you begin to glow. Having someone say, "Wow, that color looks great on you," can't help but make you feel good. Comments like these can give you confidence, and having inner confidence can give you the determination to improve in other areas. I need to thank Jean Joseph, an image consultant from California, for helping me with the information you'll read in this chapter.

I received this letter from a girl who heard people around her talking about color and wanted a simple way to understand it:

Dear Barbara,

I have a problem trying to find colors that look best on me. I am tired of wasting my money on the wrong colors. Also, how would I find samples of my colors for an inexpensive price? I'm enclosing a photo of myself so that maybe you could look at it and tell what colors would look good on me. What color of makeup should I wear? I really do want to improve myself in every way. I would appreciate it so much if you could give me some advice. Please, please write back.

The prom is coming up, and I especially want to buy a dress in the right color.

Love always, Madison

Dear Madison,

The prom! No wonder you're interested in color. Learning about color is so much fun, and understanding which colors look best on you will make a difference.

When you were conceived, one tiny miracle occurred along with the hundreds and hundreds of miracles going on to create your body. A gene harmonized the color of your skin, hair, and eyes with either a blue or a golden undertone. You will have this undertone all your life. A blue undertone is termed "cool," and a golden undertone is "warm." You must be one or the other.

Now, imagine that you're going to paint copies of the same picture on two separate canvases. One canvas has been covered with a blue tint, the other with a golden tint. All the other colors you put on top of these tints are going to be affected by them. For example, pink placed on the blue canvas will become lilac, but on the golden canvas, it will become peach. If you want to look your best, you will choose shades of color that harmonize with the color nature put on *your* canvas—your skin, hair, and eyes. If you have a blue undertone, cool colors like pale pink, royal blue, emerald green, gray, pure white, or jet black look best on you. If you have a golden undertone, warm colors such as teal blue, olive green, gold, bright yellow, or brown will look good. You can actually wear almost any color. It's the shade and intensity of that color that count.

The wrong shades can deepen and emphasize lines and minimize everyone's best feature, the eyes. If you wear makeup and clothing in shades that enhance your undertones, your complexion will look like it is glowing, your eyes will stand out, and you will look more beautiful. It is as if someone turned on a flattering light.

So, if you know the answer to the question, "Are you warm or cool?" you can always choose the most flattering colors. To help discover which you are, try this little test. Try on an outfit with your back to a full-length mirror. Turn around. Ignore the style of your clothes, squint your eyes slightly, and glance at yourself. Does this color seem to go with your hair, skin, and eyes? Does your skin look light or yellowish? Do your eyes sparkle, or do they appear to have dark circles? Do blemishes and freckles show up more?

Another way to learn your best colors is to notice when people compliment you. Do people say you look nice whenever you wear light blue or pink? Or is it when you wear bright shades of green or yellow that people comment? If you get compliments every time you wear light, pastel colors, then you are a cool. If you look absolutely great in olive green or gold, then you're a warm.

A Few Rules about Color

These days just about anything goes as far as clothes are concerned, but you can't escape the fact that some colors look better on you than others. Here are a few things about color to keep in mind:

1. Color can camouflage imperfections.

2. If you want to appear taller, wear outfits of one color. If you want to look shorter, wear separate colors on top and bottom.

3. Never wear dark nylons with light-colored shoes. Don't ever wear nylons that are darker than your clothes.

4. Your natural hair color is best. If you need to color it, go lighter, never darker, which can make you appear "hard."

If you discover you have warm undertones and you have a closet full of pastels, don't throw anything out. There are things you can do. Start by adding things that are better colors for you. For example, if you have a pink dress and you should be wearing warm colors, add a bright jacket or vest. If you have brown pants and should be wearing cool colors, wear a powder-blue shirt or something pink with them.

Keep your best colors nearest your face. For example, if a black sweater makes you look sick, be sure to wear an ivory or off-white shirt under it so your best color is showing closest to your face.

About Makeup Colors

You can also tell your skin tone by putting foundation or base makeup on and checking which tones flatter you and which don't. Cool-colored foundations are pink beige for light skin and rose-toned beige for medium to dark skin. Warm-colored foundations are sunlit beige and golden beige. Ask the salespeople at the cosmetic counters in the department stores to help you figure out your skin tones. They usually have some training in it and may offer to do your makeup for you. This service is usually free.

Blush and lipstick: Cool tones should wear mauve pink to burgundy. Warm tones should wear warm coral to rusty brown.

Eye shadow: It's best to stay very natural. Don't use any strong colors. Stay with natural tones like pinkish grey for cool or warm brown for warm.

Once you know which colors look best on you, it will be easier to make decisions since many styles of clothes often come in a variety of colors. It's such a simple thing, but it makes a difference.

Have fun, and thanks for writing.

Love, Barbara

P.S. When you go to a store, try different clothes on in the category you suspect you might fit, and do the mirror test to see which colors make you look lighter and more alive.

Samples of the two color categories:

WARM	COOL
Apricot	Light pink
Daffodil yellow	Banana yellow
Teal blue	Royal or cobalt blue
Olive green	Emerald green
Gold	Silver
Vanilla beige	Pure white
Brown umber	Jet black

Chapter 17

For Gorgeous Hair, Read On

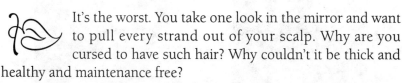 It's the worst. You take one look in the mirror and want to pull every strand out of your scalp. Why are you cursed to have such hair? Why couldn't it be thick and healthy and maintenance free?

Nothing can make you feel worse about your looks than having a bad hair day. Someone should make a law against it. You've just about decided to cut your hair all off and wear it really, really short, but then you see someone with long, straight hair to her waist and you decide to let yours grow.

Your hair, like most everything else, reacts to the care you give it. But there are things you can do without having to spend a lot of money or time.

I got this letter from two girls from Mexico complaining about their hair:

Dear Barbara,

I am writing today to ask you some questions about hair. (Actually I'm writing for my friend Elena also.) I have naturally curly hair that everyone else is jealous of, but I would be happy to change with anyone because my hair is very hard to control. Any ideas?

Elena has the opposite problem, and she just wondered how she could achieve a really curly look, or one of those styles with big, soft waves. Also, we both want to know what to do about split ends. (Neither of us want to cut our hair because we're both trying to grow it out.)

And how can we make our hair look shinier and grow faster?

Thank you for taking time out of your life to listen and help.

Love, Alicia

Dear Alicia,

Thank you for writing. It is fun to know that teenage girls all over the world have the same hair problems. Let's tackle your questions one at a time.

1. What can I do with my naturally curly hair?

Try straightening it. The key to straightening curly or wavy hair is to blow-dry it in small sections. Clip most of your hair on top of your head. Start at the bottom. Using a large round brush, lift your hair. While drying it, pull gently with the brush. Dry hair completely before going to the next piece. Work from the bottom up.

2. How can I get waves or curls into my hair?

To create waves: After shampoo-ing, bend at the waist and comb your hair so it hangs toward the floor. Blow-dry until almost dry. Stand straight up again. Take individual sections of hair, spritz with setting lotion, and roll onto large rollers. When all your hair is on rollers, finish blow-drying. Don't brush too much after you take the rollers out.

To create curls: Begin as above, blow-drying hair upside down until nearly dry. Section hair into small pieces and spritz with setting lotion. Using a small- to medium-barrel curling iron, hold the iron vertically and twist so that your hair coils around the iron. Hold each section for ten seconds.

3. What about split ends?

Sorry, but there is really only one thing to do for split ends—cut them off! You don't have to cut much, and your hair will look so much nicer. You should actually trim your split ends about once every three months.

The best thing to do about split ends is prevent them by condi-tioning your hair after every shampoo. Also, avoid rubbing wet hair vigorously with a towel. Just blot the water so it doesn't drip. Your hair is at its weakest when wet, and excessive rubbing can cause strands to split. Use a wide-toothed comb to gently detangle damp hair. Keep your blow-dryer at least four inches away from your scalp, and always keep your dryer moving.

4. How can I have shinier hair that grows faster?

The secret to healthy, shiny hair is what happens inside your body. Your hair is simply an outgrowth of your skin and scalp. It is not made of live cells, but you can affect its condition, thickness, and rate of growth by the healthy things (nutrients) you eat. For example, if you go on a starvation diet, your new hair is starving too. It will be weak and grow unevenly. It may even break off. If you eat junk food and too many sweets, it will show up in your skin and hair. Eat well-balanced meals each day. Your hair will love you for it.

To add shine to your hair, go to the beauty supply store and look for a product called a shine complex, or a product to defrizz and add shine. Hair mousse, gels, and spray weigh your hair down and take away the shine; a clarifying (deep-cleaning) shampoo will do wonders in putting back shine because it takes off all the old build-up left by conditioners and gels. Use it twice in the first week to start with, and once a week from then on. Don't do what I once did and use deep-cleaning shampoo all the time. My hair got so dried out that it looked like straw.

Brush your hair correctly. Use firm, regular strokes and avoid ripping the brush through your hair. Too much brushing can make your hair too oily. After washing, drying, and setting, gently brush and smooth hair into place.

Watch out for rubber bands. Use those special coated bands called ponytail holders. If you use decorative barrettes or combs, don't put them in too tightly.

Watch out for sun and chlorine. When out in the sun, wear a hat when you can. Tip: You can put conditioner in your hair and leave it in until you go back inside. Also, shampoo chlorine and salt out of your hair immediately after swimming.

To find the best hairstyle for your face shape, the best thing to do is consult a professional. If you don't know where to go to get a good haircut, be brave and ask someone whose hair you like where she got it done. Or you can call the beauty shop and ask for a consultation. A consultation should be free of charge, so keep it short. If you like the stylist and what he or she is saying, schedule your appointment. However, if you feel intimidated and can't communicate with that stylist, look for someone else.

Here are a few styling ideas for long hair:

The Top Knot: This is a great way to deal with growing out your bangs. It also adds a little height to the top of your hairstyle.

Step 1. Make a part straight up from each ear going across the top of your head. Gather this section of hair and twist it a few times.

Step 2. Make a small, flat bun on top of your head. Make sure the coils go around each other.

Step 3. Lift the coil up a little and flip it over so the top of the bun is against your head. Pin in place with a couple of hairpins.

The French Twist: This is a wonderful classic style. It works best with shoulder-length hair.

Step 1. Gather all your hair into a low ponytail.

Step 2. Slowly lift the ponytail straight up, twisting your hair the whole time, to create a roll running up the back of your head.

Step 3. Twist the end and fold it back down and tuck it under the roll. Once all your hair is tucked away, make sure it stays that way with a few long hairpins. This style is simple but elegant.

The Demi-Twist: This is a variation on the French Twist. It's softer and works well on curly hair.

Step 1. Gather all your hair into a low ponytail.

Step 2. Lift the ponytail straight up, twisting the whole time. Leave the ends loose. Secure with a few long hairpins.

Step 3. If your hair is curly, fluff it up a little. Or curl it with rollers or a curling iron before doing the twist.

The Pony Wrap: This looks fabulous on smooth, straight long hair.

Step 1. Start with a plain ponytail. Slip a finger through one layer of the elastic ponytail holder. Then separate a strand of hair out from the underside of your ponytail.

Step 2. Wrap the strand around the ponytail once or twice. Pull the end of the strand down through the section of elastic your finger is holding open.

Step 3. Adjust the strand so the end hangs down hidden under your ponytail and the strand covers your ponytail holder.

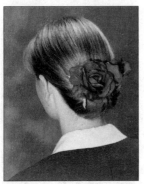

The Gibson Tuck: This is a great style for when you want to look dressed up.

Step 1. Pull hair back into a loose ponytail. With your fingers, part hair down the middle of your head from the crown to the ponytail holder. Pull the two sections apart above the ponytail to make a pocket.

Step 2. Fold the entire ponytail up and gently tuck it down into the pocket. Make sure it is tucked as evenly as possible.

Step 3. Push the ponytail holder down into the pocket as well so that it is hidden. If it won't go, loosen the ponytail a bit more. Comb carefully to smooth.

The Basic French Braid: This looks good for everyday or for going fancy.

Step 1. Gather a section of hair from the top of your head. Divide into three sections. Cross first the right section, then the left section, over the middle section to begin making a braid.

Step 2. Add hair to the right section that is now under the braid and cross the whole thing over the center section.

Step 3. Now add hair to the left section that is now underneath the braid. Cross it over the center section. Repeat until all hair has been gathered. Secure with elastic ponytail holder.

The Rope: This style is particularly great for really long hair.

Step 1. Start with a ponytail. Divide into three even sections.

Step 2. Twist the right section of hair to the right and cross it over both of the other strands.

Step 3. Twist the section that is now on the right to the right and cross it over the other two strands. Repeat until all hair is coiled. Secure with elastic ponytail holder.

I hope some of this helps answer your hair questions. I want to give credit for much of my information to Barbara Palmer, San Francisco's leading color/stylist, and to Wendy Adamson, my daughter, who I think is the most talented stylist in the country.

Thanks again for writing.

Love, Barbara

P.S. I thought you might like to see some photos of girls who have sent me pictures showing them before and after they changed their hairstyles. See what you think.

before

after

before

after

before

after

Chapter 18

Working toward Great-Looking Skin

Don't you just love how beautiful and smooth a baby's skin looks? But as you grow up, your skin grows up too. And if your family has a tendency to get pimples or acne, chances are you will get them.

There is good news and bad news. The good news is that eventually you should outgrow your teenage acne. Also, there are new ways of treating severe acne that can improve your skin immensely. The bad news is that you may have to suffer through some days when you don't look your best.

I received letters from two girls asking for advice about their skin:

Dear Barbara,

My problem is that I'm super shy. I think I know the reason I am shy. I have this bad complexion (zits everywhere). It's going away a little, but I can't stand it. I'm embarrassed to show my face. What can I do? Please send me some advice.

The other letter said:

I'm writing to know if you could give me a few tips. I want to know how to make my face look better without makeup. (I am prohibited from wearing makeup.) Also, you wouldn't happen to know how to get rid of zits?

Love, Alice

Dear Alice,

I have to tell you a "miracle story" about your letter and a letter I received from another girl on the same day who was also worried about her skin. I was reading the two letters on an airplane.

After I read the letters, I was thinking, *I wish I were a doctor so that I could really give these girls an answer.* Just then the stewardess asked over the plane's loudspeaker, "We have a slight emergency—is there a doctor on board?"

The gentleman sitting next to me raised his hand. "I'm a doctor, but I may not be the kind of doctor you are looking for. I'm a dermatologist."

A dermatologist!

When he returned to his seat, I said, "I'm so sorry to bother you, but I overheard that you are a dermatologist."

"Yes," he responded.

"Well," I said, "I just received letters from two teenage girls asking for help with their complexion problems—you know, zits."

He smiled. "We call them eruptions."

"Oh, sorry." I had to smile back. "Could you please tell me what I should tell them?"

So here is what he said, in an outline form:

1. Acne or blemishes (eruptions) are mainly genetic. In other words, the tendency to have acne is passed on to you from your parents' genes.

It can also be caused by:

A. Stress.

B. Cosmetics. Make sure that the cosmetics you use say *non-comedogenic* on the label. This means they won't form blackheads.

C. Foods rich in iodine. These foods are raw fish or shellfish. (Cooked fish is okay.)

D. Scrubbing skin too hard with a washcloth or buff pads. You can spread your blemishes and may cause scarring by scrubbing too hard. You need to wash your face gently.

2. *Chocolate does not cause acne.* Although eating healthy foods and drinking lots of water makes you healthier all over, acne is not caused by one particular food, even greasy foods.

3. *There are some solutions to common skin problems.*

A. Wash your face with a topical wash or gel. (You can get these at any drugstore.)

B. Be sure to use sunscreen, even in the winter. Get one that is waterproof, noncomedogenic, and has a high SPF number.

C. Use acne products with benzoyl peroxide as the main ingredient. (You can buy these at the drugstore.)

D. Use Retin A at night. (Retin A is a prescription topical antibiotic.)

E. If none of the above solutions work for you, make an appointment to see a dermatologist.

I need to thank Dr. Philip Hellreich of Hawaii, a Fellow at the American Academy of Dermatology, for his expert advice.

Over the years, as I have been teaching girls how to take care of themselves, I have given this little quiz to help girls determine their skin type. Get out a pencil and circle the number of the answer for each question that describes your face most accurately.

Skin-Type Questionnaire

Even though you wash your face, do you still have:
1. Oily or greasy shine all over.
2. Oily shine on forehead, nose, and chin.
3. Glowy shine on forehead, nose, chin.
4. No shine.
5. Dull-looking skin.

Do you have problems with blemishes:
1. At least half of each month.
2. Usually during one week of each month.
3. Intermittently.

4. Hardly ever.
5. Never.

Do you have clogged pores:
   1. Usually, but widely scattered.
   2. Often, especially on the nose and chin.
   3. Occasionally, mainly on the nose and chin.
   4. Hardly ever.
   5. Never.

Does your face usually feel:
   1. Bumpy under the surface.
   2. More smooth than bumpy.
   3. Smooth.
   4. More smooth than flaky.
   5. Flaky and parched.

During the winter, does your skin:
   1. Show no seasonal change.
   2. Seem a little less oily.
   3. Occasionally feel dry and tight.
   4. Usually feel tight, dry, and occasionally flaky.
   5. Usually feel uncomfortably tight, dry, and flaky.

To find your score, add up the numbers you circled. Match your score to the code below. That's your skin type.

   5-7   Oily
   8-12   Moderately Oily
   13-17 Normal
   18-20 Moderately Dry
   21-23 Dry
   24-25 Dehydrated

What does this mean? If you know what skin type you have, you can buy the right kinds of products to use on your skin.

Here are a few more things I have learned over the years of working with teenagers and their skin problems:

   1. Eruptions usually show up on your nose, forehead, or chin area because this is the oiliest part of your face.

2. Do not use an oil-based soap (read the label).

3. Never go to bed with any makeup left on your face.

4. Gently use a facial scrub once a week. You don't need to buy anything special; you can make it yourself in the kitchen. All-Bran cereal or cornmeal or oatmeal mixed with a clear facial soap works well.

5. After cleansing your face, apply a toner or astringent. A toner is for normal to dry skin. An astringent is for oily skin. (These are sold inexpensively in drugstores or grocery stores.)

6. Always put on an oil-free moisturizer with sunblock to protect your skin.

7. Keep your hair off your face. Bangs especially can cause problems.

8. Hair spray can cause eruptions.

9. Keep your hair clean.

10. Change your pillowcase often.

11. Never use a powder puff or makeup sponge over and over without washing it.

12. Never pick your face with your bare fingers. If you must "pop" a blemish, use a tissue.

13. Always use a clean washcloth when you wash your face.

14. If your acne persists or gets worse, see a dermatologist.

Be patient. Your skin will get better as you get older. Try not to be too self-conscious about your skin problems. Most of your friends like being around you for who you really are. And you certainly are not alone. Having "eruptions" is one of the hard things about being a teenager, but you will be okay.

Another thing you may be interested in is wearing makeup. I have a few suggestions that I have learned from makeup artist Debra Dietrich.

1. Use a foundation makeup that matches your skin color as closely as possible. Make sure you apply it with a sponge and blend it in at the hairline and around the jaw area.

2. To set your foundation, use a translucent powder applied with a large, fluffy brush. Translucent powder also gets rid of the shine.

3. Concealer is used to cover blemishes. Pat on and blend with your finger. Apply after foundation and before translucent powder.

4. For eyeliner, don't use liquid. Eyeliner pencils give a much softer look. Another great idea is to apply a very dark eye shadow at the lash line with a small, wedge-shaped brush. Eyeliner should be blended for a smoky effect.

5. Eye shadows should enhance your eyes. Use pale pink to brighten your eyes. Dark gray applied very lightly looks fantastic on girls with brown eyes. Smoky gray goes well with cool skin tones; for warmer skin tones, try caramel and cocoa brown. You can even apply a little bit of your blush in the crease of your eyelid for a more natural look.

6. Use clear mascara on your eyebrows to give them shape and keep wild hairs under control. Tweeze unwanted hairs under your brow line.

7. Curl your lashes before you apply mascara. Use mascara on both upper and lower lashes. Brown or brown/black is less harsh and more pleasing. Hold a folded tissue between your lashes and skin. Voila! No mess.

8. Don't overuse blush. Apply very lightly, and use natural shades. Apply only to the "apple" or round part of your cheeks. And remember to blend it back toward the opening of your ear.

Some Problems and Solutions

I don't like the color of my new lipstick. I had to waste money and throw it away.

Try layering your new lipstick with some other colors you have on hand to come up with something you like.

I have dark hair on my upper lip.

Here are three ways to solve your problem:

Waxing. Buy a waxing kit at any drugstore. Follow the directions carefully. It lasts two to six weeks.

Tweezing. Plucking the hairs one at a time is slow but easy and cheap. It lasts about one week.

Bleaching. Use a little hydrogen peroxide to lighten hair and make it less visible. Lasts about two to six weeks.

My mascara clumps in my lashes.

Invest in a little lash comb or use an old toothbrush. Work the teeth down between your lashes nearest their roots and gently comb.

I want thicker lashes.

Using a small brush, dust your lashes gently with translucent powder after you apply mascara. Allow it to dry for a few seconds, then add a second coat of mascara. Be sure to use your lash comb to separate lashes.

My eye pencils break when I try to sharpen them.

Put them in the freezer for fifteen minutes before sharpening them.

Plucking my eyebrows hurts.

Try numbing the area first. Hold an ice cube to your brow for a few seconds before tweezing. Always pluck in the same direction as the hair is growing.

Of course, you don't need to wear much more than mascara, a little blush, and some lip gloss when you are in your teens. Also, you don't need to spend a ton of money on makeup. The most expensive brands are often not any better than the regular brands. And remember, less makeup always looks better than more. If you think you have on too much makeup—you do!

I hope some of this advice helps. Remember that you have lots of people who care about you, including me.

Love, Barbara

P.S. What if everything fails and your only alternative left is to see a dermatologist, but neither you nor your parents can afford it? I know that doctors are very compassionate people, so why don't you look under "Doctors" or "Physicians" in the Yellow Pages of your telephone book. Then look under the subcategory of "Dermatologists." Pick one who is in your area and go to his or her office. You could tell the receptionist your problem. If you are too scared, you could even write a letter to the doctor, which you could hand to the receptionist to deliver to the doctor. A doctor may agree to let you pay the bill over a longer period of time when you get old enough to hold a job. Put a snapshot or a school picture in with the letter; then be prepared to wait. I can't guarantee what will happen, but it's worth a try.

Chapter 19

D.I.E.T.

The

Dynamic, Invigorating, Energizing Training

Program

A word of warning: Contrary to the exciting pictures you will see in this book, I have a serious word of caution before you even start reading this chapter. *There are no free lunches!* There is no easy way to lose weight.

I get so many letters from young women asking for a secret, foolproof formula. There *are* plans that work, but they do require work.

Here are just a few samples of the letters I have received requesting help with losing weight:

Dear Barbara,

I decided to write you and ask for some advice. I am about twenty to thirty pounds overweight. My parents are both on diets, and they simply count fat and calories. Both have lost weight, but I can't seem to do the same. I go for about two weeks eating healthy foods, and then I become very tempted and end up eating something fattening. It is so hard! If you can possibly tell me a "plan," I would be so grateful.

Dear Barbara,

I have high hopes that this letter will get to you, because I sincerely need your advice. I'm overweight, and every time I look in the mirror, I don't exactly think of myself as pretty. My problem is in the bottom of my hourglass, as you put it when I heard you speak about two young women. Would you please tell me the plan that you gave to them? I want to be in shape so bad I can taste it. Please help me. I know that with your advice, I can accomplish my goal. Lately, I've been trying to cut down on what I eat, and I'm exercising more. I want to lose some of these pounds and turn them into muscle.

I have always been kind of shy. The last time I was really into sports, I was in seventh grade. Now I want to go out for some high school sports, and I want to be more healthy. If you would give me some advice, I would truly appreciate it.

Dear Barbara,

I have a problem with weight. I'm not fat, but I'm overweight, and every day I seem to gain a little bit more. It really gets me down, and my self-esteem is slowly dwindling. I'm depressed almost every day because it's usually all I think about. I try to eat good foods, but somewhere along the line, when I start doing really well, I fall off and go back to my regular eating habits. It's really discouraging.

Losing extra pounds is hard, but it can be done. A friend of mine from Wyoming did it, and so can you. I met Brynn at a youth fireside when she was a sophomore in high school. I looked at her and thought, *What a pretty girl.*

When I met her, I put my hand on her face and said, "You are so beautiful." She almost started to cry. She blurted out, "I just hate being fat. Can you help me?"

I sent her a booklet, but I didn't hear from her until four years later. She wrote, "Sister Jones, I've lost about eighty-five pounds." She had made up her mind that no matter what it took, she would work toward being the best she could be in every way. She had followed the advice in the booklet and had been successful. She isn't perfect yet (who is?), but feeling good about herself helps.

I asked Brynn to write a letter that I could send along with mine to some of the girls I hear from who are worried about their weight. Here's what Brynn wrote:

Dear Friend,

I understand with all my heart where you are coming from. When I was eighteen years old, I was at my heaviest, 198 pounds. I was so incredibly miserable. As I sit here and think about how I compared myself to others, I can remember thinking if I just lost weight, the guys would pay attention to me and all my problems would go away. I remember how unhappy I was and how I pulled away from everyone and everything. I hated to go to school because nothing fit, and I would wear my coat every day, hoping it would help hide how fat I really was. I don't think I wanted to admit or come to the realization that I was overweight. I would go shopping and buy clothes a couple of sizes too small, thinking that just maybe by next week I would be able to fit into them. (What a joke!)

During high school, I would walk down the halls and think as I saw other girls, If only I was that skinny, I would ask guys to the dances. I would hear all the time, "Too bad she is so fat, because she is so cool, and has such a great personality. The best one was, "She has such a pretty face, but she is just so big."

I tried everything with my clothes to make myself look smaller, but now that I sit back and reminisce about that time, I realize I missed out on so much. On weekends, I didn't want to go out with my friends because I was always the biggest one, so I would stay home watching television and would end up eating even more and putting on more weight.

I felt like I was always on a diet or going on some weight-loss program, but I wasn't losing weight. I just kept putting more on. I was so unhappy with myself that everything I did, I did only halfheartedly, and I was never a success. I was always giving up.

Then, after my senior year, Barbara Jones came to Salt Lake

City and invited our Young Women group to her hotel room at the Red Lion to listen to her speak about her book, The Inside Outside Beauty Book. I didn't want to go because I felt like I didn't have anything to wear. But my mom talked me into it. After Barbara spoke to us, she was signing our books, and, of course, everyone was eating pizza except me because I was dieting. Barbara came up to me and asked why I wasn't eating, and I was so embarrassed, but I said I was trying to lose weight. Barbara put her hands on my cheeks and said to me, "You will be a huge success." I burst into tears, and I have never forgotten that moment.

Some time went by, and I was trying to diet but with no success. I finally wrote Barbara and asked for help. She sent me her winning formula, which was to focus on spiritual, mental, and physical health. I sat down and made out a game plan. I knew there were no free lunches, and that it wasn't going to be easy. It was only going to be worth it. I decided to make lists of what I needed to do in each area, and then I got started.

I knew that I needed to grow spiritually, and if I did this with Heavenly Father by my side, I would make it. Don't get me wrong and think I followed my plan to a "T," because I'm not perfect. I had bad days. I started out small in each area and worked on those goals. For example, I would run past three mailboxes, and then the next day I would run past three more. But I made sure I exercised every day, even if only for twenty minutes. I think I was waiting for some miracle to happen, and that one day I would wake up and be skinny, but I realized it's something you really have to work at. I really watched what I ate. When I would go out, I would have things cooked without butter or sauces. I realized I could not deprive myself if I wanted something. I would take one or two bites, because if I didn't, I would stuff myself with that item and eat much more than I needed or wanted.

Once I started to lose weight and fit into different clothes, it started to be exciting. So I would work out even more. I drank tons and tons of water. I started to look a lot better, and I felt like I had energy and could accomplish anything.

It did take a good six months, but I'm now working diligently on getting toned. I know this will always be a lifelong *battle for me, and it isn't easy, but it's so worth it. Believe me when I say my heart goes out to you, and I know how difficult it is and the emotional problems you go through because of this, but if I can give any advice, it is to do it for yourself, to become healthy, not to lose weight. You will have your Heavenly Father by your side. He will strengthen you!*

Then just do it!

Love, Brynn

Brynn before

Brynn after

Everyone is different. I know you have seen it even among your friends. One girl can eat everything in sight and still stay skinny. Another can eat less than her friends and still gain. Your metabolism (that's what decides how fast your body will use the energy in food) is largely decided by your genes. If your family has a tendency to put on weight easily, you will too. If your family members are usually on the thin side, then it is highly likely you'll also be thin.

But don't give up. Your situation is not hopeless. There is something you can do. The thing that affects your metabolism the most is how much exercise you get. In fact, exercising every day can make a difference in how fast your body uses up the fat that it has stored.

If you truly need to make a change in your weight, I know you can do it. It would be best if you discussed how much you need to lose with your doctor. If he or she says you're just fine, then you need to skip the next chapter and be sure to read the one on eating disorders. Be willing to accept the truth about yourself. That's what the Lord would want for you.

But if you do need to lose some weight, there are some things you can do. Read on, and remember: You are strong enough to do it for yourself.

Love, Barbara

P.S. Here are five things to remember when you're starting to change your food habits.

1. Attitude. How do you view food? Is it entertainment, or something you need as fuel to keep your body running? Eat healthy. Pick foods from the major foods groups every day. Then don't feel guilty about an *occasional* dessert.

2. Exercise. Do something every day. And forget all about the saying, "No pain, no gain." If there is pain, you have done too much. Walk, run, swim, bike, or play tennis. Get involved in exercise that is fun, and keep it up. Start easy and do a little more each day.

3. Healthy image. God created you, and he wants you to be happy and satisfied with the way you look. He doesn't want you to set unrealistic goals. Remember that most models in commercials and on television are very tall, so they tend to look lean. Stop comparing yourself to artificial images. The photos in magazines have been retouched. No one, not even the model in the picture, looks in real life as perfect as the finished photo looks. If you have to, quit looking at magazines and change channels on television during the commercials. Be realistic.

4. Expectations. It's impossible to be super perfect. Everyone makes mistakes. Remember that Jesus was the only perfect person. If you are under too many demands, talk it out with your parents or teachers. You need to be realistic about what you can accomplish.

5. God's temple. You're a temple (read 1 Corinthians 3:16–17). What kind of job are you doing of keeping the Lord's temple in good repair? If the Lord is important to you, you can honor him by eating right and keeping your body healthy.

A Plan That Really Works

I have a friend, Susan Ward, who has made a tremendous change in her life through her own perseverance and courage. I asked her to write you a letter telling what she accomplished. Here it is:

Dear Friend,

I would like to tell you a little about myself—how I lost weight and improved myself not only on the outside but on the inside as well.

Life was hard for me when I was growing up. I never felt good about myself, and I definitely didn't feel pretty. Kids at school made fun of me. Sometimes I would come home and cry and cry.

One day, I challenged myself to work my hardest to lose weight. I had set goals before, but somehow this one was different. I knelt in a long prayer with my Heavenly Father and poured out my whole soul to him. I told him how much I hurt inside because my self-esteem was so low. I promised myself and

Heavenly Father at that time that I was willing to change my life forever.

It was hard. I walked for an hour each day. That was really hard. Afterwards, I collapsed on the couch. But the more I walked, the easier it grew, and then it became fun! Before, when I felt lonely or bored, I would eat, because eating gave me something to do. What helped me not to overeat was when I met the neatest girl, and she became my best friend. To have a friend who loves and encourages you, no matter what, is just the best. It is amazing what a word of encouragement will do. Suddenly, I realized I could lose weight. The only person who could stop me was myself, and I'd never thought of it that way before. I've heard it said that we only fail when we have given up. I loved new days because I knew if I faltered in my resolve the day before, I could start brand new again.

I ate a very low-fat diet. I did not starve myself, which was the mistake I had made MANY times before. I ate a lot of fruits and vegetables and grains. My favorite food is spaghetti, and I ate a lot of that. I walked a lot and jogged a bit every day. I remember the first time I jogged for ten minutes straight. I was so excited! I did aerobics also. I found some fun tapes, and that made it a lot easier to be consistent. I found that exercise is vitally important. It not only helps you lose weight, but it makes you feel good about yourself.

My life has changed so much. I am so grateful to my Heavenly Father. I know I couldn't have done it without his help. I know it! I love life, and now I know anything is possible.

I have lost over 100 pounds and six dress sizes, and today I feel something I have never felt before—I truly believe I am of worth. To feel beautiful and to love yourself, both on the inside and the outside, is fantastic. Life is wonderful! Change and improvement are essential to becoming the beautiful daughters our Heavenly Father knows we are.

Love, Susan Ward

Susan is looking and feeling great. She now has the confidence to go out into the world and talk about the things she believes.

Susan before

Susan after

Here's a paragraph from the note I got from her while she was at the Missionary Training Center getting ready to go on her mission to Russia.

Dear Barbara,

I feel like I have really grown up and realized a lot of things. I don't think the Susan three years ago could ever successfully have gone on a mission because I was so self-conscious and afraid of everything. I have learned that we should not be afraid of life but live life to its fullest. I have learned that if we go to the Lord in honest prayer and express a righteous desire, and then work at it with all our might, we can do all things.

Can you see the tremendous changes Susan was able to make in every area of her life? She learned to recognize the beauty she possessed both inside and out.

Let's go back to the starting point of her changed attitude. Susan stressed that in trying to lose weight, she didn't starve herself. Let's never use the word *diet* again, because DIETS DON'T WORK.

Garfield the cat says, "Diet is die with a t."

And did you know that *stressed* is *desserts* spelled backwards?

To make a real change, you have to change your way of thinking. This time you are *not* going on a diet. You are just going to adjust your way of eating—forever. You are going on the Dynamic, Invigorating, Energizing Training program. Tell your friends you're sick of feeling tired and not having enough energy, so you've decided to get into healthy eating.

And how are you going to get into a healthy mode?

EAT, DON'T STARVE
BREATHE
MOVE

Eating is important. You have to have fuel to drive a car. Your body needs fuel or food to keep you going.

But what kind of food? Let me tell you a story to illustrate. Recently I was on a fifteen-hour nonstop flight to Australia. Before breakfast was served, the flight attendant was counseling some passengers on how to handle this long trip. She said: "Now, if you want to sleep, you'll order the French toast and sausage, because after you've eaten all of the toast with its syrup, you'll experience a slight energy surge. But then you'll crash and go right to sleep. You see," she continued, "the syrup (pure sugar) will give you a short burst of energy, but then your blood sugar will drop below normal, and you'll be tired and sleepy. Also, the sausage has so much fat that your body has to work overtime, and all of your energy will go to trying to digest the fat. Follow my advice, and I guarantee you'll sleep."

To really have energy that lasts, keep your intake of sugar down. For example, if you eat a jelly doughnut at ten in the morning, by noon you'll be starving, maybe even weak and shaky.

And go easy on fat. I knew a girl who led a busy life. She would fix her own lunch every day, and, because she was in a hurry, each day that lunch consisted of a cheese sandwich. Then when she got home after a long, hard day of school and work, she wanted to eat something quick and easy. She would make another cheese sandwich. Eventually she started feeling ill and having all kinds of health problems. When she went to the doctor, he asked her about her diet. She told him what she ate. He said she had the symptoms of malnutrition. Her illness and lack of energy were caused by her terrible eating habits.

Only 15 to 20 percent of our calories should come from fat. Fat has more calories per gram than carbohydrates and proteins, so it only takes a small amount of food to really pile on the calories.

So, the next time you're starving and you catch yourself nibbling on potato chips or ordering even the child portion of frozen yogurt, remember that you could stuff yourself on pasta or baked potatoes for the same amount of calories and feel full and satisfied. You don't always have to choose brown rice over ice cream, but you need to eat the excellent or good foods much more often than the bad or not-so-good foods.

Now that you've seen two of the big culprits in a bad diet—fat and sugar—look at the chart on the next page to see some food choices and how they rank for nutrition per calorie.

The secret in using this chart is to eat things in the Extraordinary, Excellent, and Good columns. Avoid foods in the Not So Good and Bad columns, or at least use them very sparingly. Even with the proper foods, moderation is a key word. Pay attention to the size of the portions in everything you eat.

Make a Plan

Unlike most diet books, I am not going to give you a menu to follow or a schedule for your day. That's up to you. Select foods from the Extraordinary, Excellent, and Good lists. Exercise (pick something you like to do) every day. Drink lots of water (eight glasses) every day. And stay busy with things you like to do. Most of all, be patient. This takes time, but persistence pays off.

Following are some tips to think about as you're making your own action plan.

Keep your portions small. It is very important that you don't overeat. Measure all your foods. One serving of fruits, vegetables, beans, or grains is about 1/2 cup. For fish or chicken, a serving should be about the size of the palm of your hand.

Concentrate on the things you *can* eat, instead of moaning and

Extraordinary	Excellent	Good	Not So Good	Bad
sprouts	skim milk	sugar-free Jello	salad oils	pudding mixes
brown rice	tomatoes	lean lamb	fried fish	peanut butter
soybeans	mushrooms	pears	fried chicken	salted snacks
fish	strawberries	sugar-free	lobster	white flour
sweet potatoes	apricots	pudding	sausage	soda pop
bran	corn	eggs	scallops	regular mayon-
pinto beans	green peppers	veal	margarine	naise
kidney beans	oranges	eggplant	cheese	cake
lima beans	white potatoes	artichokes	sour cream	olives
garbanzo	bananas	pineapple	pizza	bacon
beans	squash	vegetable juice	honey	french fries
peas	papayas	celery	butter	candy bars
oats	cabbage	watermelon	oysters	soup mixes
spinach	cantaloupe	whole-grain	cream	regular hot
broccoli	cucumbers	bread	canned fruits	dogs
	grapefruit	cherries	dried fruits	sugared
	onions	rhubarb	granola	cereals
	carrots	low-cal fruit	avocado	chocolate
	cauliflower	juice	raisins	regular ice
	brussels	fat-free mayon-	regular cottage	cream
	sprouts	naise	cheese	sugar
	peaches	low-cal salad		pie
	nonfat yogurt	dressings		potato chips
	apples	nonfat hot		salt
	chicken,	dogs		pickles
	skinless	nonfat cheese		most fast food
	tuna, packed			
	in water			
	turkey,			
	skinless			
	raspberries			
	lettuce			
	pasta noodles			
	white rice			
	nonfat cottage			
	cheese			

lamenting about the things you can't. Your attitude makes a big difference.

Salad bar tips. Many girls who think they're eating right can't figure out why they're not losing weight. Sometimes the real problem is foods that you think couldn't be that bad for you, but they really are. A salad bar is a perfect example. You think you are eating all these things that are great for you. But if you slather on the dressing and sprinkle bacon bits, croutons, raisins, or cheese on top, then your "healthy" salad has more calories, especially from fat, than a hamburger and fries.

Here's a tip from a friend of mine who, through exercising and watching what she ate, went from a size 18 to a size 6. She says she always asks for the salad dressing on the side. Then, before taking a bite of salad, she dips the tines of her fork partway into the little dish of dressing. This way she tastes the dressing but uses only a small portion of what she'd get by pouring it on.

Drink plenty of water. As part of your healthy eating program, you'll need to have a water bottle handy. Get used to carrying it with you all day. A good hint is to freeze the water in your bottle. As it melts, you'll have nice cold water. Make sure you get eight to ten glasses (80 ounces) a day.

Water helps everything in your body work better. It makes your skin look better. And it keeps you healthy and functioning at your best.

Start moving. Always remember that daily exercise is important. As you start exercising, do just twenty minutes a day. Add five minutes each week until you've reached your goal of a forty-five-minute workout. Don't skip your exercise except when you are ill, and don't ever overdo it. If you exercise too much, you will be defeating your goal of becoming healthy. Forty-five minutes is just fine. Don't become extreme in either the foods you choose to eat or the amount of exercise you do.

Here are some great ways to get that exercise you need. Mix and match them according to your own tastes and circumstances. Whatever you choose to do, always warm up beforehand by stretching your muscles.

1. Walking and running

Start running, and continue until you get tired. (The first day that will probably be about thirty seconds.) Now, keep walking. Once you have caught your breath, start running again. Continue this walk-and-run cycle for your full exercise period.

2. Bike riding

Start out on a regular or stationary bicycle with a warm-up pace. Work up until you are pedaling faster. If you get tired, slow your pedaling down until you catch your breath. Then continue to build up your speed once more. Distance does not matter as much as time.

3. Jumping rope

In a pinch, you can even do this without the rope. Put on some music or turn on the television and start jumping. Remember to do an easy skipping step, switching from one foot to the other. The speed is not important. Keep it steady.

4. Speed walking

Start walking as fast as you can. Do not slow down until you are huffing and puffing. Keep up your speed for as long as you can; then slow your pace but don't stop. When you catch your breath, start walking fast again.

5. TV aerobics or aerobics class

Doing an aerobics tape or attending a class is an excellent way to vary your exercise routine. Be sure the aerobic portion of the class is at least the twenty to forty-five minutes you are aiming for.

6. Exercise machines

Put on some music or your favorite TV program and start walking, rowing, or whatever. Gradually increase your speed until you feel slightly out of breath.

A Final Word on D.I.E.T.

You are a strong person. You can do anything you want to do. Don't be hard on yourself. Losing weight will not really change anything important about you, but if you know it would help you feel healthier and more energetic, go for it. What you truly are on the inside is the thing that matters.

Don't let food control your life. You have too many other great things to accomplish. At the same time as you are working on developing good eating habits and keeping up your daily exercise, work on the other things we have talked about in this book. Look for people who are doing good things. Watch for ways that people are being supportive of you and others.

You can do it, especially with Heavenly Father on your side. Remember, in the scriptures it says, "With God nothing shall be impossible" (Luke 1:37). If I could look you in the eyes for just a moment or two, I could see the incredible, beautiful person you are already.

Love, Barbara

P.S. Here are suggestions from some of the girls I have helped to train who have served as Miss USA:

Christy Fichtner
Miss USA 1986

Michelle Royer
Miss USA 1987

Courtney Gibbs
Miss USA 1988

1. Choose exercises you like. Add variety so you don't get bored.

2. Getting in shape takes time. Be patient.

3. Find low-cal desserts. Sugar-free Jello (eight calories) with low-cal whipped topping (twelve calories) is a favorite.

4. Take small bites.

5. Eat slowly.

6. Don't eat between meals unless the foods are on the Extraordinary or Excellent lists.

7. Jump rope or run in place during your favorite TV show.

8. Drink lots of water.

9. Read fitness magazines.

10. Don't beat yourself up when you slip. Just get back on track.

11. Eat breakfast.

12. Treat yourself well. Take bubble baths. Buy a flowering plant for your room. Give yourself a manicure when you feel bored.

13. No one is perfect: not beauty queens, movie stars, or cheerleaders.

14. Just keep it up.

15. Don't weigh yourself (except at the doctor's office).

Chapter 21

A Silent Cry for Help

They have big-sounding names, *anorexia nervosa* (self-starvation) and *bulimia* (eating too much and forcing yourself to purge or get rid of what you have eaten), and they are frightening and dangerous diseases. Eating disorders often start in simple ways: thinking too much about every bite of food, becoming obsessed with the numbers on the scale, wanting to be in complete control of at least one thing in your life. Then the disorder causes huge problems, much bigger problems than the little bit of extra weight.

Take this little quiz about your attitudes toward eating. We'll talk some more at the end.

Answer yes or no
1. I weigh myself every day.
2. I exercise a lot, sometimes more than once a day.
3. I've taken pills like laxatives to help "clean out" my system.
4. I'm always feeling fat in comparison to others.
5. My parents comment on how little I eat.

6. I get angry when people tell me I should eat more or gain weight.

7. I like to eat alone as often as possible.

8. I feel insecure about myself unless I am thin.

9. I feel very good about myself when I've eaten nothing or hardly anything all day.

10. I panic when someone says it looks like I've gained a few pounds.

11. I have eaten everything on the table, sometimes all the dessert, without being able to stop myself.

12. I feel in control when I control my weight.

13. I lie about what I've eaten.

14. Every time I look in the mirror, I see places where I need to lose some weight.

15. I have made myself throw up so I won't gain weight from what I've eaten.

If you have answered yes to two or more of the above questions, you might have an eating disorder. In trying to lose weight, you could be headed for serious problems that can put you in the hospital and destroy your life. This is not something to play around with. You need help as soon as possible.

I received this letter from a girl who scared me to death. I wrote back to her as fast as I could.

Dear Barbara,

I wanted to write to you and thank you for setting an example, and for helping so many people. I feel really stupid writing to you because I don't know you, and you don't know me, but maybe that's better. I want to ask your advice.

I really wish I could like myself, but there's really nothing to like. I'm pretty dang ugly, and you would probably agree with me if you saw me. I'm also pretty fat. I don't eat a lot at all, and I always watch my fat intake. I also take dance lessons. I've been taking lessons for about eight years now, but I still stink at it, and I'm the fattest one at the studio.

I have a few jobs. I work at a nursery school, at the high school bookstore, and I baby tend. I go to school and take dance *classes in the evening. I go to church. I'm a Laurel. My life is busy but fun, and I should be happy, but I'm not happy! I wish I knew why, but I really don't.*

I tried so many ways to lose weight, but I can't. The only ways I've ever lost any weight are what I tried a few months ago and what I'm doing now. A few months ago, I tried to starve myself. I only made it for nine days without any food. But, I gained it back really fast.

What I'm doing now is sort of scary. I'm afraid I can't stop. I try not to eat anything, but if I do, I don't leave the bathroom until I throw it all up. It sounds gross, and it is, but it works! I've been doing it for about a month now. I want to stop, but if I do I'll just get fatter and uglier, if that's possible.

I always try to please everyone and make them happy. I just don't know how to do it for myself. Who knows, maybe I don't deserve to be happy.

I'm sorry I ruined your day. I hope you can write back. Thanks for taking the time to read this letter through.

Love, Lynn

I was extremely frightened. Lynn had clearly been caught up in eating disorders. As you can see from her letter, she doesn't value what she really is inside. She is involved in all these wonderful things, but she thinks that if she can change one little thing on the outside, it will somehow change everything else in her life. It won't.

This is the beginning of the letter I wrote back to her:

Dearest Lynn,

Thank you for writing to me. When I received your letter, I said to Heavenly Father, "If only I were a trained counselor . . . " But I know that God does hear our prayers, because in my papers I found this letter that I had saved for some reason. I am sending it to you; I think it will really help.

And here is the letter I had saved. I just thought it was amazing that I happened to have this very letter and that I was able to find it so quickly. I want you to read it too.

Dear Barbara,

You probably don't even remember this, but during BYU Education Week this past year, I spoke to you about some of the problems I've had with eating disorders (mainly bulimia). You told me that if I wanted to, you'd like me to write down my experience and send it to you.

I don't want other girls to end up like me. I don't want them to even contemplate it. I want to give them a strong warning. It is all I can do to help. I've had many other struggles this year, making me realize how important the gospel and the Lord are in my life. I can't see how anyone lives without the Lord by their side.

During the middle of my freshman year in high school, I was 5'7" and nearly 160 pounds. I was bound and determined at that time to lose weight. I wanted people to see that I wasn't just a chubby little girl, that I had the courage to lose weight. So I began to exercise and eat a little less. I found that I actually felt a little better about myself because of my efforts.

After a while, the weight began to melt off. Not being satisfied, I began to exercise even more and eat less than I already was. By the time summer was over, I was down to 136 pounds. That was a really good weight for me at my height, but I still felt fat. I felt as if everyone was looking at me, that the muscle I had developed from exercise was really fat. The words used to tease me through the years echoed in my head.

I continued to work out and lose weight. I walked around school with a constant scowl on my face. I remember a guy coming up to me and saying, "You have such a pretty face. How come you never smile?"

I was stunned. Did I have a pretty face, or was he joking or being mean? I talked myself into believing he was being rude. About that time I began eating next to nothing. But still the results weren't satisfying to me.

After a while I yearned to eat. My mother is an excellent cook. So when I did eat, I'd eat as though it was going to be my last meal in life. Right after, I'd get on the scales and just bawl. Then I started to throw up. It took me a couple of times just to learn how.

At that time I had become friends with some really neat kids. The Lord was with them. I remember looking in the mirror and cutting myself down. Why was I always so tired? Why was my hair always so oily? Why had my face broken out so bad? I remember wishing my nose wasn't so wide, that my eyes were a different color, that my hair could be as straight as a model's. Everything seemed to be wrong. Why did anyone even acknowledge my presence?

School seemed like just a daze. I was always so tired; my efforts seemed to be failing. I was truly wrapped up in myself. I was so worried that if I gained weight, I'd lose all the great friends that I'd made. I didn't even think about my family, who were, at the time, under great financial stress.

One day, after I'd thrown up, I got on the scales. How could I gain weight? No way, I thought. How could this happen? I nearly picked up the scale and smashed it into a million pieces. No! I didn't want to be teased again. I didn't want that insecure feeling to return. I was so devastated. How could I live? I figured I needed to exercise more, but hard as I tried, I couldn't. I'd get so tired.

My friend Andrea found out one day about my bulimia. She wasn't the only one who had noticed. I had very good friends, friends who watched out for me and knew of some of my eating habits. My friend Shirley also knew. She was a senior and kind of just took me under her wing. She was the kind of person you know you have met in the preexistence. She was the big sister I never had. She knew me. I don't know how, but she did. Shirley had a neat spirit and was very close to her Father in Heaven.

Shirley noticed that I hardly every ate, and when I did, I usually went to the bathroom right away. One day she asked me if everything was going all right in my life. She said I looked tired all the time and seemed to have something else on my mind. I told her I hadn't had enough sleep and that was it. Shirley wasn't fooled but didn't say anything. In the back of my mind, I knew she was someone who I might be able to tell.

One day, after I had thrown up, I took a good look at my face in the mirror. My eyes were bloodshot and had dark circles under them. My hair hung in a greasy mess. I usually saw my double chin that seemed to hang on me. This time I saw something different. It was like looking at a face I'd never seen before.

Who was this person? It scared me—I who had everything and was throwing it all away.

For some reason, I decided to tell Shirley. When I told her, her face became stern. "I knew there was something wrong with you," she said. Then, very kindly, she asked me how much I did it. I told her once or twice a week, which wasn't the truth. It was more.

"Well," Shirley said, "you need help so you can quit. Why don't you tell your mom?"

I hit the ceiling in anger! There was no way I would be able to tell her. She had other, more important things to do with her time. Plus, it would break her heart into pieces. She would tell me things I already knew, that I was being selfish.

Shirley suggested that I pray and ask for help. Prayer? When had I quit praying? No, I couldn't. My answer would be exactly what I didn't want to hear. I was afraid to go to the Lord and ask him for help. Yet I missed the feeling I had had when the Spirit used to be with me.

Shirley turned out to be a good person to trust because she kept things to herself. But she did confirm some of my friends' suspicions, which meant a lot of people had noticed and hadn't let on.

Finally, it came down to me. I had to decide. This was so out of control that I had a very hard time keeping anything down. I sat on the floor of the bathroom and cried, "Lord, please help me." I begged, "Help me." Then a feeling of peace came over me, and for the first time in days, I slept that night until morning.

The next week, I tried hard not to throw up, but every day I seemed to have to start over. I couldn't control my body anymore. I began to get scared. Again I prayed for strength, courage, and understanding parents.

I asked Shirley to be with me when I told my parents. Shirley drove up. There was no backing out now. As we waited for my mom's full attention, I looked into her unsuspecting face. How could I do this to her? How could I tell her? I took a breath and blurted it out. "Mom, I've got a problem. I can't hold any of my food down because I've been throwing it all up!"

I could barely get the words out. Shirley grabbed my hand and said to my mom, "Amy needs your help to quit this!"

My mother's face filled with anger. "Are you looking for attention?" she demanded.

I burst into tears, "No, I can't quit. I keep throwing up more."

Of all her children, I had seemed to be without problems. Mom looked at Shirley and said, "I think your friend needs to leave now."

Shirley didn't budge. She pleaded, "Amy needs positive reinforcement."

My dad took it differently than my mother had. He was very compassionate. It surprised me. I thought it would be the other way around. They instantly wanted to shove food at me. I began to cry because of how sick food made me. During that weekend, my parents learned the seriousness of my problem. They didn't allow me to be by myself. Someone was constantly watching me. I spent a lot of time in my room praying or sitting there thinking. The friends who knew called me and included me in their prayers. The Lord was my comfort. He seemed to be there, sitting next to me or cradling me.

My dad was a loving support. My mother, on the other hand, hardly spoke to me. I felt as if she was trying to block me out of her life. This hurt me so much. I could hardly stand to be at home.

About a week later, my dad had to go out of town. I was in my room trying to sleep. My mom came in and sat down by my bed. She didn't just cry, she bawled. "I can't believe you've done this. You're not even pretty anymore. You're ugly. You're not my beautiful girl."

"Mom, I'm sorry. Please don't hate me," I cried.

"Oh, I don't hate you. I love you! Put yourself in my place once and see how you'd feel."

Then she hugged me, and we both cried. I felt some relief. At least she was talking to me again. All of my prayers were being answered. My mother was understanding me.

At school I was constantly being hugged, and a lot of people were watching out for me. I couldn't believe all these people cared about me! My home teachers came over to give me a blessing, since my dad was out of town. The Spirit directed these men to bless me, to heal and help me with all my problems. It was the *most spiritual blessing I'd ever had. That Sunday, a lot of my friends fasted for me. Some even told me they had never fasted totally but had this time for me. And I had thought I was worth nothing to anyone! I never felt so loved. In time, with a lot of faith, I became better.*

About a month later, one of my friends committed suicide. He was a boy I'd once been best friends with. We had chosen different ways to live and had grown apart. Still, I had a great love for him and was crushed when he died.

Attending his funeral was an experience I'll never forget. The funeral home was packed with teenagers, all devastated by his death. Some old friends I hadn't seen for a while showed up looking nearly dead themselves. Did he know how many people he was hurting? To most of them, he was gone forever.

I realized who I was and what I was to do. I am a chosen daughter of God, and I know of Christ and his sacrifice for us all. The Lord has a plan for me, and I want to do what I know is right. God has given me this body, and it's up to me to take care of it. A great happiness has stayed with me ever since then.

My dear friend, please remember who you are and what really counts in life—learning to love yourself and to please the Lord.

If you already have a problem, please tell someone. Ask your bishop for help or go to your school counselor. If you can't tell them, then write it in a note and give it to them. Most importantly, know that your Heavenly Father loves you and is waiting for you to call upon him. He will help you. I can promise you that.

And even though I don't know you, I want you to know that I love you too.

Love, Amy

Our Heavenly Father gave you a miraculous body that can be used to bring you much happiness and to allow you to accomplish many good things in your life. To do this, it truly is not important that you be thin. You should work toward being healthy. Exercise every day, but for no more than forty-five minutes per workout (or longer if you are playing a sport that is stop-and-go). Eat healthy foods every day. Don't skip meals. And stick your scales in the closet. Don't weigh yourself at all, ever. Numbers don't mean much. What is best for one person isn't even close to being good for another. Only weigh in at the doctor's office, and then you can ask them not to tell you your weight.

If you have to, give up looking at fashion magazines or pictures of models. Pictures lie. No one, not even the model who posed for the picture, looks that perfect. Television shows and movies are made simply to entertain you. If watching them makes you think that is how the world should be, or makes you feel bad about how you look, don't watch them.

If you take all the time you are now spending worrying about your weight and feeling awful about yourself, and focus it on others instead, you will see a miracle happen. You will feel better, you will be more happy, and others will think you are great. Your Heavenly Father will be there for you. He will comfort you in your sad times and carry you through your tragedies. He will be your friend during the times when you need someone to lean on. And even though you may wish that little things about your life were different, relying on him will bring you great joy.

If you think you might have an eating disorder, tell your parents or someone in your ward. They can help you find professional help.

Love, Barbara

P.S. If you have a friend you suspect may have an eating disorder, here are a few things you can do to help:

1. *Understand.* She may not even know she has a problem. She will be defensive and deny what you have observed or try to explain it away. Be gentle when pointing out unhealthy eating habits.

2. *Love her.* Remind her that you are still great friends.

3. *Find help.* Tell an adult, like a guidance counselor at school or her Young Women leader or the bishop of her ward. If you try to help her by yourself, she may reject your suggestions. She won't do this as easily with advice coming from an adult.

4. *Explain.* Be realistic about food. Remind her of food's nutritional value and assure her it's okay to eat.

5. *Be trustworthy.* Don't tell her secrets unless they are destructive. Don't nag her. Just remind her that you're there to help her fight her battle.

6. *Pray.* Ask Heavenly Father to help your friend with her problem.

Part 5

Making Good Choices

Dear Barbara,
Sometimes I just feel so hopeless.
How can I know that Heavenly
Father cares about me?

Satan's Three Great Lies

Sometimes I imagine that when we are tempted, it's like having a little angel sitting on one shoulder, whispering in one ear, and a little devil sitting on the other shoulder, yelling into that ear. While we are trying to decide what to do, the angel keeps saying, "Don't do it. Don't give in."

But the devil is telling us lies. Here are three of the biggest lies he tells us:

"Once won't hurt."

"No one will know."

"Everybody's doing it."

As our prophets and leaders have told us over and over again, we can't do wrong and feel right. It is impossible! Years of happiness can be lost in one foolish moment. But Satan would have us believe that happiness comes as we surrender to his enticements to self-indulgence.

Here is a letter I received from a girl who learned the hard way that falling for Satan's lies only brings misery:

Dear Barbara,

One Friday night, some friends and I went out on this guy's land and had a party. There was beer there, and I started drinking. We were all having a great time by this huge bonfire, talking and dancing.

A few of us decided to go back to this guy's house and get our cars. It was about 9:30, and I rode back with my boyfriend in my friend Joe's truck. Joe had been drinking. We had all been drinking. Joe was driving way too fast, and we were all listening to really loud music. There was this one hairpin turn that has to be taken at about five miles an hour. We were approaching that turn, and everyone started yelling at Joe to slow down. He didn't. The truck rolled.

I can still feel us suspended in the air, deadly silent. It seemed to take forever. Then the truck hit the ground. The sound was so loud, and it rolled so fast. I could feel my head hitting the windshield.

It's weird, the things that go through your head. As we rolled I thought, "It's not my time. I'm not ready. I have to go to college, get married, have kids." Worst of all, I was scared that I might die, and I'd been drinking, and I knew it was wrong. I didn't even know why I had done it, but I didn't want to meet my Father in Heaven this way. I never had more fear in all of my life.

An ambulance came, and then I knew I was really hurt. I threw up over and over and over again. I don't remember the rest of the ambulance ride. My doctor was called, and he didn't even recognize me. My eyes were swollen shut. They were like huge silvery balloons. My jaw was hanging off to one side, and I couldn't close my mouth. After X-rays, they found my jaw was broken in three places and my skull in two. I had air in my brain, which is very dangerous, and they weren't sure I would ever have my sight again.

I don't want to drag this out, so I'll sum everything up. My jaw is wired shut for six weeks; my teeth are all messed up; my memory and concentration are very slow. The thing that affects me most is that I'm permanently deaf in my right ear. My balance has been affected, and I have yet to see what I am with that. But I'm so grateful to my Heavenly Father that I'm going to be okay. This accident has helped my attitude about life and obstacles that we face. My family and I are very close now. My relationship with my Father in Heaven has grown immensely.

Barbara, I remember when you taught us about Satan and his lies. I even remember what they were: (1) Once won't hurt; (2) Nobody will ever know; and (3) Everybody's doing it. But it just seems like when things start happening, you think, Oh, it could never happen to ME!

Please write back to me. I appreciate your friendship soooo much!

Love, Susan

P.S. Please share what happened to me to help any teenagers. Maybe they'll be stronger, and Satan won't get to them like he got to me.

Dear Susan,

What a horrible accident you've been through! I'm so glad that you are going to be okay. And thank you so much for giving me permission to share your letter.

I was speaking to teens in Newcastle, Australia, about Satan's lies, and I felt prompted to tell your story. When the talk was over, a very nice-looking man dressed in a navy blue suit came slowly walking to the podium trying to gently guide his teenage daughter down the aisle toward me. The girl's name was Leah Harker. She was eighteen years old, and she could hardly walk. With each step, she struggled, clinging tightly to her father's arm.

When they finally reached me, she painstakingly began to speak. "Si . . . Sister Jones . . . I . . . I . . . really . . . en- . . . en- . . . joy . . . your . . . talk! The . . . doc- . . . tors . . . tol . . . me . . . I . . . would . . . never . . . wa- . . . wa- . . . walk . . . again." (Her head was shaking back and forth as she spoke.) "But . . . la . . . look . . . at me . . . . I'm walking! I wa . . . wa . . . want . . . to . . . be . . . a . . . missionary . . . som . . . day."

Her father whispered to me, "Leah was much like the girl, Susan, whose letter you read tonight. She had gone on the wrong track with a bad group of friends. She wouldn't listen to us, her parents. She left home, and then she had her accident."

Leah suffered a brain injury following a head-on collision in her car. She needed an eleven-hour surgery to reconstruct her face, as almost every bone had been fractured. Eight plates and 118 screws were later used to repair her injuries. She was in a coma for six months. She had suffered a lack of oxygen to the brain at the scene of the accident. She has lost the ability to read, walk properly, and talk clearly.

Leah's father and mother shared these photos with me and have given me permission to use them.

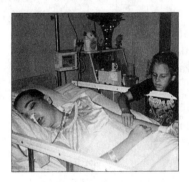 

Before the accident, Leah had a promising career as a horseback rider and was the winner of many trophies and ribbons in numerous competitions. But her main desire in life had been to serve a mission. Then she fell for Satan's lies.

Another teenager wrote a letter to me and enclosed several poems. Here is one. When you read it, you'll understand the problems she created for herself when she listened to Satan's lies.

Never Stand Alone

So many times they'd warned her,
Of a dark and sinful zone,
To keep it to a friendly date,
And know you're not alone.

She felt she needn't worry;
She had the truths they'd taught.
She'd never know the hole she'd dug,
The entrance Satan sought.

Her foolish pride did blind her
To the warning that they gave.
Her only hope, a heartfelt plea
For the virtue she must save.

The self-control she valued
Soon left when face to face.
The apple of her father's eye
Now sat in cold disgrace.

She'd tried to do it all alone
Despite pleadings from above,
But came to know she couldn't stand,
Without the Lord's true love.

For this girl, the devil's lies led to a horrible experience. She is struggling to become again the clean, pure girl she once was. She discovered that Satan led her carefully away from the truths she had been taught, then left her comfortless and abandoned. Now she has turned her life around through the repentance offered by our Savior. This young woman is making progress, but she wishes with every fiber of her being that she had listened to what she knew was right and not to Satan's lies.

"Once won't hurt."

"No one will know."

"Everybody's doing it."

These lies lead to nothing but pain, heartache, and sorrow.

Susan, I know that you have the strength to turn your life back to the Savior. You have had a hard lesson on how Satan's lies can lead to such devastation. Please write to me and let me know how you're doing. I really care about you.

Love, Barbara

P.S. I saw these ten Teen Commandments on a plaque hanging on a friend's wall. I don't know who wrote them, but they are a good guide to keep you from falling for Satan's lies. Read them every day if you hear that little devil shouting in your ear.

1. Don't let your parents down; they brought you up.
2. Choose your companions with care; you become what they are.
3. Be master of your habits, or they will master you.
4. Treasure your time; don't spend it—invest it.
5. Stand for something, or you'll fall for anything.
6. Select a date who would make a good mate.
7. See what you can do for others, not what they can do for you.
8. Guard your thoughts. What you think, you are.
9. Don't fill up on this world's crumbs; feed your soul on living bread.
10. Give your all to Christ; he gave his all for you.

There Is a Way Out

In the last chapter, we talked about three lies Satan uses to persuade us to make mistakes. This leads us to another big lie that Satan would have us believe in his attempt to destroy us. He tells us that if we *have* made a mistake, there's no way out. We are finished. There is no way we can be forgiven. He would like us to believe that things are hopeless and that there is no use trying anymore to be righteous.

If we believe this biggest lie of all, then we don't understand the atonement of Jesus Christ. The truth is, no matter what we have done, we can ultimately be forgiven. We will have to endure pain, sometimes a lot of pain, and take some difficult steps to straighten out the situation, but it is possible for us to repent and put our lives back together.

Here is a letter I received from a girl who fell for Satan's lie:

Dear Barbara,

Last year, when I was sixteen, I met a young man, a non-member, at a volleyball activity. He was twenty. When I first laid eyes on him, I knew that he was suffering spiritually, and I wanted to help him. I've never been very popular. I'm definitely not cute, and I'm mildly overweight. However, I do well in school, play the piano, and am good at tennis. So, I've always focused on my personality and my talents, accepting guys as just good friends, and thinking that the rest would come in due time.

This young man and I started seeing each other, and my main goal was to give him new hope and a new set of glasses to see the world through. Obviously, he saw my light shine because he asked me to go steady. I was surprised, but I figured if that was what would help him the most, I'd do it. I knew he smoked and drank occasionally, and I suspected that he had lived with a previous girlfriend, but I knew my morals and was preparing myself for the returned missionary that I would meet one day. I wasn't worried. I considered it a service project! I didn't even worry about crushing his heart because I knew he had a bad temper, and the hurt wouldn't last extremely long.

We went on dating this way for a few months, and he was improving tremendously. Then one night, he was over at my house, my family was gone, and we were watching videos. It happened! I just don't even know how it happened. I won't include the details, but I awoke the next morning with the shock that I had lost my virtue, my chastity. I became very confused, flustered, and sick at heart. I didn't know what to do, and I didn't know how to break it off. My parents had warned me against this relationship so many times that they finally just got tired of talking to me about it.

I then tried to accept the fact that I was ruined and resigned myself to a future with him, because I know there is no turning back the clock. There is just no way out. My soul is in torment. My life seems to have gone from bad to worse. I miss my closeness with my Heavenly Father. I'm just not sure he's there for me anymore. Maybe he got tired of trying to get through to me, like my parents did. I don't know how to reach him anymore.

Please, please write soon.

Love, Veronica

Dear Veronica,

I am grateful that you wrote to me, but I am very, very sad to hear what you have been going through in your life. I hope that things will get better for you. The most important thing I want to talk about is something you mentioned in the last paragraph of your letter. You said you felt there is no way out. You said that your soul is in torment and that you miss your closeness with God.

Heavenly Father hasn't gone anywhere. He's still there waiting for you to come to him. Do you believe in Jesus Christ? If your answer is yes, then don't you believe him? Christ says, "Come unto me, . . . and I will give you rest" (Matthew 11:28). He says, "I will never leave thee, nor forsake thee" (Hebrews 13:5). Again, he says, "Peace I leave with you, my peace I give unto you: not as the world giveth, give I unto you. Let not your heart be troubled, neither let it be afraid" (John 14:27).

These are promises he makes to you! Don't you believe him? Get on your knees and talk to Heavenly Father. He will hear you.

Yes, you do have weaknesses that have gotten you in trouble. We all do. But remember this scripture, "I give unto men weakness that they may be humble; and my grace is sufficient for all men that humble themselves before me; for if they humble themselves before me, and have faith in me, then will I make weak things become strong unto them" (Ether 12:27).

I read a story the other day that illustrates this principle perfectly. It was in Stephen Robinson's book *Believing Christ.* It was a story about an old man named Bob. Bob was a rugged coal miner and a good man. He raised his kids in the Church, held family home evenings, paid tithing, and supported his children on missions, but because he could never quite handle all of the commandments, especially the Word of Wisdom, he never attended church.

One night he had a dream. He dreamed that he was standing on the edge of a cliff and Jesus Christ came riding up to him on a horse. Around the saddle horn was draped a big rope. In his dream, Jesus said, "Bob, I want you to tie this rope around me and my horse and lower us all the way down to the bottom of the cliff."

Bob said, "It would be impossible for me to lower even one of you to the bottom of the cliff, let alone both you and the horse."

Jesus handed him the rope. "Bob, I said tie the rope around the horse first and then around me and lower us to the bottom of the cliff."

So, being obedient, Bob did as the Savior told him. He tied the rope as instructed and carefully lowered them all the way to the bottom of the cliff. Then the Savior looked up at Bob and said, "Now drop the rope."

Bob immediately dropped the rope, and the Savior gathered it up and looped it around the saddle horn. His parting words to Bob were, "Never forget, it is almost impossible to do all the things required of you on your own power, but together we can do all things."

Christ is there for you! He says all you have to do is knock. He loves you so very much. He is just waiting for you. I promise you that if you will trust the Lord and take the first step, there is a miracle of forgiveness waiting for you.

A few weeks after receiving your letter, I got a letter from a Young Women president about one of her Laurels, who had been involved in a date-rape situation. Now the girl was afraid she was pregnant. She didn't want to tell anyone, so she was taking all the guilt, pain, and responsibility on herself. She was tormented because she was carrying all this around inside, just as you said you were doing. She kept saying, "I can't tell. I'll never tell. There is no way out. There is just *no way.*"

Well, I know a way! Christ says, "I am the way" (John 14:6). Satan will always try to get you to believe that you are hopelessly stuck, but you never need to be afraid. No matter what happens in your life, Christ will be there to guide you back if you will reach out to him.

You are a child of God. You have his divine nature, and you have the atonement of Christ that pays the price for your sins and errors.

Now, go talk to your bishop. It may seem scary, but you can do it. Imagine getting rid of the fear, guilt, and sadness you are feeling now and having that replaced by a sense of peace, confidence, and happiness. Don't fool yourself by imagining that if you just wait long enough, or confide your problem to a close friend, or pray hard enough, you can make your pain go away. It doesn't work that way.

The Lord has an "agent" in the bishop. He is the one authorized to guide you through the process of repentance. He will help you in a spirit of love and kindness.

How do I know this? Read this letter:

Dear Barbara,

I want to thank you with all my heart for answering my let-ter. I want you to know that I was really scared to go in and talk to my bishop. I wasn't even planning to call him for an inter-view.

A few days later, I got a call from him. He wanted to talk to me. It wasn't time for a birthday interview or anything like that, so I was very worried. I went to his office and sat down. My heart was beating so hard and fast, I felt like he could read my thoughts. He asked me all the usual questions and then almost got up to shake my hand good-bye, when he asked me if I were morally clean in all aspects. That is when I started bawling! And I mean really hard. I was so embarrassed, but he listened without saying a word. I told him exactly what John and I did.

After I was done, I felt as though I had been released from prison. I feel so much better now. I feel like a 100-pound weight has been lifted from my shoulders.

What I need to do from now on is be very cautious and pick young men who put Heavenly Father at the top of their list and respect others. Thank you so much for reading my letter. I couldn't talk to anyone else. Now I don't have to. "Though your sins be as scarlet, they shall be as white as snow" (Isaiah 1:18).

Thank you for having faith in me.

Love, Adrienne

Veronica, I promise you that you will not be left alone. You have been given a guide to help you tell right from wrong. Listen to those promptings. "For behold, again I say unto you that if ye will enter in by the way, and receive the Holy Ghost, it will show unto you all things what ye should do" (2 Nephi 32:5).

I love you. I know that God lives, that he knows your name, and that he loves you too. Through him you can find the way out. You can start over. You can become clean again.

Love, Barbara

P.S. Christ is the answer, the bridge from here to there, the solution to the great dilemma. "Ask, and it shall be given unto you; seek, and ye shall find; knock, and it shall be opened unto you: For every one that asketh receiveth; and he that seeketh findeth; and to him that knocketh it shall be opened" (Matthew 7:7-8).

This is the good news of the gospel.

Chapter 24

Does God Really Hear Our Prayers?

Before I joined the Church, I went through some really hard times in my life, especially in my marriage. I was married at age nineteen to a young man who suffered from manic depression. A manic-depressive person is nice and normal one minute, and then a destructive dragon seems to take over the next minute. Thank goodness, with today's medical advances, there is help for these people.

When I was just a newlywed, I found my husband on the floor of the bathroom after he had swallowed a whole bottle of aspirin tablets. He had to be rushed to the hospital. Another time he took all my scrapbooks outside to the backyard and burned them!

But those incidents were nothing compared to the two times he held me with a loaded gun pointed at me, and I figured that my life would be ending at any second. What did I do during those two scariest times in my life? I called out to God. In the silent depths of my mind, I asked, "Heavenly Father, are you there?" And both times I heard his words of comfort, silently speaking to my spirit, saying, "Yes, Barbara, I am here." Knowing he was there with me gave me so much comfort, and I felt total peace. Both times, that peace just made the tears stream down my cheeks, and nothing else seemed to matter. My Heavenly Father was with me!

I am sure Heavenly Father had more for me to do in this life, because both times, my life was spared. Because of these experiences, I have always given the challenge to teenagers to test what I have found to be true. The scriptures say, "I am with you always, unto the end of the world" (JST, Matthew 28:19).

Get down on your knees and ask, "Heavenly Father, are you there?" Then wait—listen. You will hear in the silent depths of your mind, "Yes, I'm here." Of course, at first you'll just think, "Oh, I only *think* I'm hearing his voice because Sister Jones told me I would." Ask again. You will hear the same thing, "Yes, I'm here."

Then, carry it a little further and ask, "Heavenly Father, am I on the right track?" Now listen. He will answer. He loves you. He cares. Heavenly Father does answer our prayers in many different ways.

Here are excerpts from three letters I received from girls who did as I suggested:

Dear Barbara,

I just wanted to write and tell you I did what you challenged us to do. The next morning I got down on my knees and asked my Heavenly Father if he was there. I stayed in that position for a minute or so, and a voice said, "Yes, Becky, I am here." Then I asked, "Heavenly Father, am I on the right track?" Then after a minute or two of waiting I heard a voice saying, "Yes, Becky, you are on the right track."

You'll never know how much it meant to me to hear my Heavenly Father's voice saying what he said.

Love, Becky

Dear Barbara,

During a youth conference, you told us about your trials with your first husband and how silently you prayed.

For several years, my parents had been fighting or separated and fighting. For five years I cried constantly, and for the last two I just couldn't cry anymore. Sometimes I wonder how I ever lived through it.

It's been almost two years since my parents' divorce. It has been thirteen months since I joined the Church. This year my father is to be married in the temple to a wonderful woman.

Sister Jones, I know my Heavenly Father is there. I asked him if he was, and do you know what he said? He said, "Yes, yes, of course, and this is where I will always be."

Love, Rebecca

Dear Barbara,

I got back home [from a youth conference] on a Wednesday, and my dad had to be rushed to the hospital on Thursday where he stayed in intensive care for over a week. The cause is still unknown. The doctor only called it a raging virus. As I sat in the front seat of the ambulance next to my mom, I thought my dad was going to die. For the first time in my life, I faced a very critical situation. So, I did what you did when you were scared. I asked my Heavenly Father if he was there. He very plainly and clearly said to me, "Yes, I'm here, and it's going to be all right."

My dad came home and is fine. I am closer to my Heavenly Father now more than ever. I learned to appreciate my parents. I now know for sure that Heavenly Father does hear and answer prayers.

Love, Trudy

Dear Trudy,

God *does* hear and answer our prayers in many ways. Sometimes you will hear the still, small voice telling you what to do. At other times, your prayers may be answered through a person—maybe your parents, or a friend. Still other prayers may be answered through a song or a story or the scriptures. You can hear the Lord's direction all around you.

I mentioned earlier some of the trials I experienced in my first

marriage. Some time after I left that situation, I met and fell in love
with a wonderful man, Hal. One day I said to him, "You're my hero."
"No, I'm not," he answered. "I'm just a regular old human being with
feet of clay. I think you better get right with God." I listened to him.
I wasn't a Latter-day Saint at that time, having been raised in the
Catholic church, so I started going to Mass every single day.

I met a nun and asked her to teach me about the Bible. The first
day in the convent, she opened the Bible to Jeremiah 1:5, where it
said, "Before I formed thee in the belly I knew thee."

I thought to myself, *You did?* This was my Heavenly Father,
someone I wanted to know.

My teacher taught me about a man named Jesus Christ who
said, "I am the way, the truth, and the life: no man cometh unto the
Father, but by me" (John 14:6). At that time, I began a prayer that
would not be answered for five years. Every single night I prayed,
"Jesus Christ, who are you? Where are you?"

Then, in the summer of 1979, my husband and I ended up in
Salt Lake City during a vacation. We walked into the visitors center
and watched a film there. The very last image on the screen was a
picture I had never seen before. It showed the Savior surrounded by
angels, wearing his white robes with a red sash around his waist.
There in the darkness, he said to me, in the depths of my mind,
"Barbara, here I am. Come follow me."

He *is* there. He said, "I will not leave you comfortless" (John
14:18), but don't forget that he also said, "I, the Lord, am bound
when ye do what I say; but when ye do not what I say, ye have no
promise" (D&C 82:10). In other words, you have to be doing your
part. You have to be willing to do as the Spirit guides. You need to
have faith that your prayers will be answered, even if the answer is in
the negative.

If you continue to live as closely as you can to the good things
you have been taught, then miracles—yes, I said *miracles*—will happen in your life too.

You'll be in my prayers.

Love, Barbara

P.S. You may be saying, "Well, this is really nice for you, but I've never had Heavenly Father answer any of my prayers in those ways." If you try the following exercise, I think you will discover how often the Lord is watching out for you:

Get a small notebook. On the cover write: *My Notebook of Miracles.* In this notebook, write down all the small things that happen in your life every day.

For example, when you're feeling down and your friend calls just to ask if you want to go get an ice-cream cone, that's a little miracle.

Notice when your family comes to watch you perform with the choir, or when your Young Women leaders give you a special assignment that really helps your testimony grow.

All these little things are tiny miracles. They aren't just coincidences. Your prayers and concerns are being answered through other people. And sometimes you will be the one who is the means of answering someone else's prayers. When you have a feeling or an impulse to do something for someone else, follow those feelings. The Lord may be working through you. You might be helping in some of his miracles too.

When you write them down, you will notice that you are not left on your own. You are surrounded by angels.

A Note to You

Dear Reader,

My last words are to you, yes, you, *the girl reading this book.* I tell you with all my heart that I know that your Heavenly Father loves you beyond words. You cannot even begin to imagine how special you are to him. You are his daughter! I know that Jesus Christ lives, and there is absolutely nothing in your life that you cannot handle with God and Christ as your allies.

But also, please know that I love you! Yes, even though I may not know you personally, I think that you can feel my love for you throughout the pages of this book. I am your friend. And if there is any problem I can help you with that wasn't in this book, please write to me. I promise that I will write back.

Here's where you should send your letter:

Barbara Jones
Dept. YW
10 Badger Court
Novato, CA 94949

Love, Barbara

Index